nothing bad happens in life

nature's way of success

Also by the same author:

The Mind's Mirror: Dream Dictionary & Translation Guide
The Mythology of Sleep: The Waking Power of Dreams
Tao te Ching: The Poetry of Nature

nothing bad happens in life

nature's way of success

By Kari Hohne

Published by Way of Tao Books.
P.O. Box 1753 Carnelian Bay, Ca 96140
PaperBird is a division of Way of Tao Books.
www.wayoftao.com
Printed in the United States of America

ISBN: 978-0-9819779-2-8

For Mollie, my nature fairy and teacher,
and Marisa my conservation soul mate.

Contents

Prologue 1
Introduction: The Power of Nature 5

SECTION ONE 17
The Field of Action: Principles 1-8
- Empowerment: Being Ruler of Your Empire

SECTION TWO 33
Life's Rules of Engagement: Principles 9-16
- The Laws of Nature: The Art of Living

SECTION THREE 51
Promotion and Advancement: Principles 17-24
- Leadership: Inspired by the Way of Nature

The Great Masters 71

SECTION FOUR 77
Approaching the Gateway: Principles 25-32
- Changing Perspective: Cultivating What is to Come

SECTION FIVE 99
Movement in Stillness: Principles 33-40
- Conserving Energy: Developing Power

SECTION SIX 117
Modeling Nature: Principles 41-48
- Emulating Nature: Industrious and Perfect

SECTION SEVEN 139
The Land of Te: Principles 49-56
- Inner Treasure: Claiming Your Destiny

SECTION EIGHT 159
Accessing the Great Power of Nature: Principles 57-64
- Nature's Rejuvenating Power: The Way of Success

Prologue

Success is a pathway of self-completion,

and the seed is always within you.

Walking through a field, you see a flower growing on the hillside. You admire its beauty, while wholly unaware of its leaves, opened like tiny solar panels to capture the sunlight. Without understanding the intricacies of this plant, you may fail to appreciate what it can teach you about manifesting your destiny.

Within its seed is a blueprint of everything it may become. As it pushes beyond the earth and rocks to initiate photosynthesis, it moves through the darkness, intuitively knowing there will be light at the end of the tunnel. Whether fruit or flower, all direction manifests from *within*. Through photosynthesis, it releases the oxygen atom from the carbon molecule. The plant thrives and yet, it nourishes other life forms in the process. By taking its place within the larger fabric, it is simply being the unique creature nature designed it to be.

On its journey, all obstacles peel away its protective covering. It pushes beyond any rocks that stabilize the soil, keeping water near its roots. The rock also forces the stalk to grow stronger, ensuring that it will remain steady through the changing seasons. In the world of nature, the rock is every bit as important as the plant.

In stark contrast to the green hillsides, its flower attracts the tiny insects that will steward its pollination process. Perhaps it will grow seeds that will use the wind, or the fur of passing animals for procreation. When the wind blows, outworn leaves are stripped away to replenish its roots. Its future well-being is dependent upon its ability to *let them go*.

The plant can teach you how all living things are dependant upon the environment for sustenance and renewal. Your environment may nurture you, but it does not define you: *that takes place from direction that rises within*.

Adaptation reveals that everything you will ever need to survive is already within you. Nothing new is added to the genetic mix, and you need only turn inward to allow experience to carve away the layers that hide your authenticity. More importantly, you need not fight the very thing that is bringing your unique nature forward.

When you meet difficulty, you may believe that life is working against you, yet something very profound has been committed to your success since the beginning. Allowing nature to become your teacher, you will discover that *Nothing Bad Happens in Life*. Without showing favoritism, nature's way is purposeful; all creatures are made stronger.

Unhappiness is a sure sign that authenticity is rising within. Whether the inner or outer landscape is stirring, the winds of change always foster suppleness and renewal. When it seems something is not right in the world, you grow unhappy. Yet, discontentment is simply your hunger pain for change.

The world of nature would teach you that *where* something is going is not as important as *how it gets there*. The plant interacts with the nurturing energy of life and as a natural creature in a natural world you too, must find your connection to what unfolds around you. In the chain of sustenance, which flows from one species to another, or in the exchange of elements that blend to become something new, nature always moves purposefully in its pursuit of *a better way*.

Just as life moves to release the potential energy locked within stagnation, anxiety is dormant energy rising to the surface to be used for productive transformation. Feelings of uneasiness subside when you recognize that something is taking place *in here* and not *out there*.

When you encounter a rock, you may believe life has blocked your way, when it is actually peeling away your protective covering *to set you free*.

Unhappiness always returns you to a pathway that is uniquely your own. When you observe difficulty as a question and obstacles as opportunities, you will see how life is always asking the same question:

Is it real?

If it is real, it will endure.

In an environment that explores novelty, being flexible ensures that you meet with no limitations. In proportion to your unwillingness to allow your real nature to find expression, you will discover the germinating power of life, ever striving to bring it forward. It is often in the things you cannot change that you discover life's power to guide you.

In a concrete world of mechanical sounds, you may forget that you are a natural creature in the river of life. When a floating leaf encounters an obstacle, it begins to move in a circle. It demonstrates the movement of *turning back*. Beyond the leaf and the obstruction is something, which seeks continual movement.

This is the great river of life.

Conflict reveals how two things, which are stuck and doing similar things always seem to meet in the great river. In this way, opposition can teach you about *your condition,* and how you become *stuck.* The potential power captured in the latent energy of the leaf as it turns in circles, reveals how you can access enormous energy by simply *letting go.* Increased power becomes accessible when you open to how life coaxes you to manifest your nature. Let go and simply fall back into the great river.

Success is a pathway of self-completion and the seed is always within you. When you open to the ways of nature, you will find yourself moving purposefully upon the tapestry of life.

By turning within, you can reconnect with life's germinating power. It is born of the same silence where a thousand seeds are becoming the landscape of spring.

Introduction

Nature provides a sanctuary for the human spirit. Immersed within its rejuvenating tapestry of colors and sounds, you can forget your battles and discover *the art of living.* Tracing the endless expanse of sky, freedom renews itself, where clouds form and evaporate on the horizon. A trout leaps into the calm surface of a lake, and all sense of time and urgency dissolves. It re-emerges in the color of autumn, growing in the blushing hillsides.

Over and above how nature renews the senses, its tremendous power for renewal is also active in each creature. Its diverse species can shed light upon the human condition, while its varied processes offer clues to the evolutionary journey common to all living things.

In pursuit of the best it might become, nature fine tunes existing traits, and is relentless in its ability to overcome any barriers to its forward progress. By exploring *Nature's Way of Success,* you can discover a natural pathway to wellness and success.

More than two thousand years ago, the ancient Chinese developed a philosophy called the *"Return to Nature."* On the threshold of our evolving environmental consciousness, their ideas are quite profound. Their appreciation for nature and its ways offers a method for approaching experience innocently to discover a more natural way of being in the world.

Unlike the ideas of the West, which explored nature from a human perspective, to the ancient Taoist *nature was the teacher*. Both set out to describe the underlying meaning of existence. While the West strove to understand the nature of *things* and *being in time,* the East was content to observe the *becoming* or *transient* aspect of how all things move together in interconnectivity.

The ancients observed life's synergistic interaction and called its regenerative thrust *Tao*. In the course of changing events, the *Way* unleashes *te,* or *Tao's* transformative essence inherent in each creature. Like all living things of the earth, you follow an *inborn* pattern of development, brought forward by the changes taking place around you. Revealed in the ways of nature is the secret of how to overcome all obstacles.

The Master said: *"One who understands the workings of nature uses no counting rods."* At all levels of life, we observe how something that appears *bad* is fundamentally *good* and necessary for renewal. A forest fire burns away old growth to prepare for the new; the same pollution that causes global warming and ocean temperatures to rise is washed away in the typhoons and hurricanes that are created. Nature's purposefulness ever reminds us *Nothing Bad Happens in Life.*

Autumn returns the seeds of rebirth to the earth, while winter incubates and nurtures the seeds. *"Nature does not give up the winter because people dislike the cold."* In the synergistic aspect of life, *one thing* can only be understood by observing what stands next to, and influences it. At the core of each experience is a thread that binds you to what you may become. This thread weaves through the entire tapestry of your existence.

Standing at the bank of a river, the Master said: *"everything flows on and on like this river, without pause, day and night."* We have a tendency to fight this perpetual flow, while we hold fast to the familiar. *"We appreciate the changes taking place around us, while wholly unaware of our own mutability."*

Life on earth has thrived for billions of years because it holds an inherent wisdom that allows it to sustain and renew itself. As we find value in what nature has done perfectly since the beginning of time, new markets have begun to trade on its sustainability. Protecting rainforests, oceans and watersheds offer valuable returns when compared to the expense of building water treatment and purification facilities.

Observing the purposefulness of what unfolds in nature, two classic books emerged that capture life's movement toward change. The *I Ching* is translated to mean the *"Book of Changes."* The Chinese word *"i"* means both, the "changes observed in nature" and something done with "ease." The *Tao te Ching* reveals how one might return to a more simple way of being in the world. As a compilation of the ideas found in both texts, *Nothing Bad Happens in Life* presents natural processes that explore crisis productively, where you can discover the *natural way* to empowerment and success.

The Power of Nature

When a warm and cold front meet, the warm air rises while the cold air descends. This movement creates a circle dance. The excited turning of opposite energy generates electricity, wind, rain and ultimately, new life. Each time opposite forces collide, productive energy is released. Long before scientists identified the diverging forces at the root of the atom, the Taoist described all manifestation as the interaction of the negative Yin and the positive Yang. They knew that without this oppositional energy, life would lose its vitality and become stagnant. Opposition is not a negative event, but the necessary way that life evolves toward harmony, dissolution and renewal.

Conflict releases stabilized energy within us that gives *charge* to a situation, which oftentimes feels uncomfortable. This sudden surge of energy can lead to a sense of crisis, which forces us to explore *new* ways of seeing *old* situations. When this *charge* is tapped as the latent source of our vital power or *te,* we recognize how experience evolves to bring our authentic nature forward.

What cannot be seen in science is observed by the behavior of something else. The gravitational movement of celestial bodies leads us to discover new planets. The Master said: *"Trees show the bodily form of the wind; Waves give vital energy to the moon."* Although we cannot see the greater force, we see how it shapes the world of events. At the root of all experience, we detect the way of Tao.

Observing change as the shifting of Yin and Yang energy, these ideas literally meant the dark and sunny side of a hill. While it is the same hill, the natural ebbing and flowing of phenomena has the effect of changing its appearance. Therefore, *"Tao is the One, which portrays itself as the negative Yin and the positive Yang. The Three emanate to become the many, called the ten thousand things."* Similarly, science describes how the negatively charged electron and positive nuclei interact to become the foundation of the many manifestations we observe.

Unlike the western idea of a deity, endowed with a personality, and whimsically organizing the world, the ancient Taoist respected how nature orchestrated order. Evolution drives life forward, exploring productive growth through diversity and friction. Natural selection weeds away the modifications that may affect our survival.

Life displays harmony in its symbiotic chains of sustenance, although anything that would block its forward progress must *give way.* The only thing of which we can be certain is that change is life's only constant.

One therefore, discovers how to access a greater power by learning to flow upon the great river of life.

Nature's Way of Success

The sixty-four principles from the *Book of Changes* can teach you how to rule your *empire* using natural processes as inspiration. Each principle is a variation of eight fundamental phenomena, which can be emulated to achieve success.

Water reveals a lesson about the power of stillness. As it meets an obstacle, it grows in volume and energy to overcome any barriers to its forward progress. Water breaks down the elements of any substance it encounters through non-action, and therefore suggests a growing strength that mounts by not *doing* anything. Also called the *Abysmal,* Water captures the unknown and mysterious depths of your *inner* empire. Sometimes a necessary deluge is required to release you back into the great river. The Chinese image of crisis combines both danger and opportunity. These concepts are inseparable from the standpoint of growth. *Crossing the Great Water* coaches you to be fearless and vigilant in approaching the changes.

Fire offers a lesson about synergy and dependence. Any flame is always connected to whatever keeps it burning. Its synergistic aspect mirrors how you are connected to a guiding source within. Through stillness, obsessions can be relinquished because without fuel, there is nothing to burn. Also called the *Clinging,* the Fire portrays how all of life is fundamentally intertwined. It becomes a role model in observing the connection between the cause and its effect.

Mountains provide perspective and are a model of constancy, or how being planted reveals the order of the world. You climb mountains to obtain a wider view and discover how *"the climb is long and difficult, but the fall is quick and inexorable."* Mountains are formed over a long period, and are the result of one land mass sliding and lifting another. The Mountain can teach you how life will lift you up when you allow the course of events to lead you. As the winds of change hone you into your most basic elements, you can stand as a monument for those you lead.

The Lake inspires a powerful peacefulness, regardless of the changes taking place upon its surface. It reveals a lesson about accessing your depths where you can discover a perpetual stillness and the source of your wellspring. Although the wind can disturb its surface momentarily, it always evens out. As inspirational virtue, *"make your heart like a lake, with a calm, still surface, and great depths of kindness."*

These four phenomena, when emulated, foster power through the virtue of stillness. By accessing your center, you can make contact with the germinating power of life.

Additionally, there are four constructive and moving phenomena observed in the world. Since the seasons changed with the roaring **Wind** and the crashing **Thunder**, the ancient Taoist observed how the natural world also fostered renewal through movement and *friction.*

Wind is the result of high and low-pressure systems coming together. It captures the idea of perpetual movement and following where the changes may lead you. Just as leaves are tugged from the branches of trees during autumn, you too, must remain open to the Winds of change to achieve renewal. Called the *Gentle,* it reminds you how success is often the result of slow and deliberate effort. Even while you push forward, you must also observe how events "push back" to give definition to your nature. The Wind portrays the virtue of purposeful activity and no matter how the climate changes, you must trust that change is necessary.

Thunder also portrays movement. It is the sound of expanding air when lightning charges through the atmosphere. Whenever you hear the sound of Thunder, you can be certain the climate is about to change. Nature ever reminds you to move beyond complacency. Thunder captures the idea of waking from a state of slumber. Called the *Shocking,* Thunder embodies the unpredictable nature of life.

The Creative is the force of Yang, viewable as observable particles or the positive forces that are active in generating life. As nature's activating and creative force, it portrays the virtue of expressing yourself in whatever way nature designed you to be. No two things in life are alike, and just like the unique flower on the hill, the Creative drives you forward in actualizing your destiny.

The Receptive captures the force of Yin. The unseen properties of waves and fields interact with the creative force to produce all that we see. Nature's unobservable manifestations however, are every bit as powerful as the visible. In nature's gestating movement toward rebirth during winter, the Receptive demonstrates the virtue of Yielding or turning back. Like all things of the earth, you turn back to be renewed.

Electro magnetism, gravity and molecules within the atom reveal the power of opposing forces. Yin and Yang are dependent upon each other and each cannot exist without the interaction of the other.

The ideas from these ancient texts reveal how success is a combination of power and receptivity. The balance between movement and stillness reveals that *"there are times to move forward and times to go within, as you move inward and outward according to fixed rhythms."*

The following sixty-four principles allow you to discover how your pathway is a blending of inspirational direction and the gentle prodding of how experience changes you.

The Master said: "The great mass of breath is the wind yet, there are times when the wind does not move. When it does move, a myriad of orifices and appendages are aroused to make sounds. Have you never listened to the sound of the wind in the cavities, mountains and among the branches of trees?

The wind blows in a thousand different ways, but each sound is produced in its own way. What is it that excites all this, and makes each way be itself, and all these things be self-produced?"

The Changes is a book

from which one may not hold aloof.

Its Tao is forever changing,

alteration, movement without rest.

Flowing through the six empty places;

rising and sinking without fixed law,

Firm and yielding transform each other.

They cannot be confined within a rule;

it is only change that is at work here.

They move inward and outward according to fixed rhythms.

Without or within, they teach caution;

they also show care, and sorrow and their causes.

Although you have no teacher,

approach them as you would your parents.

First, take up the words; ponder their meaning.

Then the fixed rules will reveal themselves.

The beginning line is difficult to understand.

The top line is easy to understand.

For they stand in relationship to cause and effect.

When it comes upon the right person,

one who has an inner relationship with life,

it can forthwith be taken

and one can be awakened to a new way of living.

-Book of Changes

SECTION ONE

The Field of Action: Principles 1-8

"In the Great Circle, there is no separation."

CH'IEN The Creative

1st Degree: *To discover life's fundamental harmony, you must first uncover your connection to it.*

"A little kingdom I possess, where thoughts and feelings dwell;
and very hard, the task I find of governing it well."

– L.M. Alcott

"The clouds pass and the rain does its work and all individual beings flow into their forms." Ch'ien is the principle of Yang and represents the idea of being empowered in life. As opportunity emerges, it may sometimes feel like a challenge. Just as circumstances bring you to maturity, life prods you when it is time to move forward.

There are times when you must be firm in standing up for what you feel you should to do, in a situation where you may feel powerless. Making the necessary changes allows you to express your full capabilities. Without the freedom to keep growing, your real nature remains arrested.

As the first principle of the *field of action,* Ch'ien describes the beginning stages that lead to fulfillment. You can no longer claim to be a "victim." Everything unfolding in the field of action is necessary for your growth. If you feel stuck, look for the closed doors funneling you toward an open door.

Empowerment comes when you discover your fundamental connection to life and how the prodding of experience always makes you stronger. Observe what unfolds as nature's way of ensuring you remain the ruler of your empire.

Meeting the world of events, your normal orientation can disconnect you from believing that you have anything to do with unfolding events. There is an inconsistency of belief, each time you take responsibility for your success, but blame events for your failure. Ch'ien demonstrates how you access life's creative energy by *what you do.* The Master said: *"you cannot plant a large tree within a small pot."* The width and depth of your beliefs mirror the growth of your branches above. *When you take inventory of your thoughts and actions, you will discover the seeds of what will grow to become tomorrow.*

Focused on growth, experience shapes you; when you shut down, life evolves to make you open. To follow the energy of life, the playing field *out there* always presents hidden treasures, or opportunities to expand your awareness *in here.* In the face of any challenge, have faith that everything is coaching your real nature forward. Ch'ien is a principle about the need for action. Once you remove the barriers that keep you from moving forward, you will experience life in more powerful and fulfilling ways.

K'UN The Yielding

2nd Degree: *Reaction is how you defend the past against the future.*

"Take rest; a field that has rested gives a bountiful crop."

– Ovid

"In harmony with the boundless, the Receptive embraces everything in its breadth and illumines everything in its greatness. Through it, all individual beings attain success." K'un is composed of all Yin lines to show how effective is balanced with a time of turning *inward.* You *"move inward and outward according to fixed rhythms"* and the unseen field *within* is your inner empire, which also requires nurturing as you grow.

When you cultivate a natural response to what unfolds, you are not defensive, and are therefore, able to observe how life teaches you. To continuously see life's beauty in its simplicity is the lifelong quest and reward of the sage. Circumstances shape your growth, although reaction is how you defend the past against the future. *A natural response means you respond to life without defending anything.*

While you may find it odd that mystics deny the reality of the outer world, more people deny the immense power and reality of the inner world. K'un suggests how beliefs shape experience. Rather than doing anything, remain still and observant. Overcoming your need to react defensively, you will begin to respond to life and allow it to pull you toward your destiny.

K'un describes the need to follow the energy of life as a witness to how you participate with it. When you open to the teacher of life, you will observe more and do less. K'un embodies how yielding or bending makes being pliable powerful. Where Ch'ien has a focus on *what* you create, K'un asks you to understand *how* you create.

The Master said: *"when closely related things do not harmonize, misfortune is the result."* When you compose your inner world and control its gusts and storms, you will discover wellness and harmony all around you. Life prods you forward, but misfortune is how *"those who go against the Way end up being called unlucky."*

When you are searching for direction, you will find it through dreams, intuition and inspiration. When inner clues are measured against events, they come to validate your pathway. There are times to push forward and times to remain still. Stand in the moment and observe your reaction to what unfolds around you. When you stop *reacting,* you will find yourself simply *doing,* and you can move forward with a new sense of ease and power.

Together, K'un and Ch'ien reveal how you find direction on the pathway of experience, and how experience comes to unleash your latent potential. To follow the evolutionary energy of life, you must first take responsibility for the part you play in blocking its ability to guide you.

CHUN Difficult Beginnings

3rd Degree: *Dragging the adversary about when there is no adversary will cost you your inner treasure.*

"Do the thing you fear, and the death of fear is certain."

– Emerson

"When the Creative and Receptive draw together, there is a time of new beginnings. Hence follows the idea of difficult beginnings." Many cultures describe a type of chaos that brought the world into existence. In the budding of new life at the onset of spring, we see the unpredictable environment that all new endeavors must immediately face. Represented as seedling that must immediately push beyond dirt and rocks to survive, Chun suggests how difficulty breaks away your protective covering.

Danger and opportunity are inseparable from the perspective of growth. Adversity allows you to see how life carves away your unnecessary layers. To be skilled in the *Way,* be fearless in approaching change; to be one with it however, you must recognize how fear masks your vital power.

The Master said: *"when you examine your heart and find no taint, what cause is there for self pity or fear?"* A heart tainted by fear projects the very barriers that reinforce self-pity. To rule the empire, you cannot have dragons lurking about.

Perseverance in the field of action comes when you can recognize why *authenticity* is more important than fear. Obstacles only take shape when you avert your eyes from the destination; in every way, they are making you stronger.

"Dragging the adversary about when there is no adversary will cost you your inner treasure." When you unmask the adversary, you will discover how having an adversary allows you to continue in the illusion that life is working against you. When you *blame something or someone else for your condition,* you remain powerless. The more you deny your power to be real, the more conflicted life becomes. However, life is seeking only to set you free.

All new endeavors embody a certain level of uncertainty. Operating without obvious reinforcement is the only way that you can find your inner direction. Something within you is being shaped by unfolding events and struggling for definition. If you cannot see this energy as being your own, you empower it in others and use it as a reason for failing.

To do the thing you fear, you must persevere like the plant that grows taller than all surrounding obstacles, with the sole purpose of pressing your *real* face into the sunlight. *Fortify your nature with a power, which cannot be threatened.*

In time, you will discover as you move less through space, you travel closer to your center. To follow the way, make peace with adversity for what it may teach you, and you will always know success.

MENG Youthful Folly

4th Degree: *To know success, you must make peace with the idea of failing.*

"No man is free who is not a master of himself."

– Epictetus

"Youthful Folly means confusion and subsequent enlightenment." Meng asks you to recognize how failure is a *prerequisite* for success in what you are doing. You must not hide your weakness, but allow experience to transform your weakness into strength. The Abysmal Water wells up at the foot of the Mountain, portraying the inexperience of a youth who seeks a wider awareness. Folly describes the false starts that come from a lack of experience, but this trial and error is necessary to season you. If you want to know success, then you must make peace with the idea of failing.

In life's pursuit of excellence, *"carving and polishing means removing the layers. Cutting and grinding is the cultivation of the self."* Meng is the symbol of something growing beneath a cover. It portrays the illusion of how you believe you must conquer others to develop power. You will find that *"you must only conquer yourself."*

Composing your inner terrain, and at peace with what unfolds, you will discover joy in all you do. Expertise may require action, although wisdom rises through stillness. Youthful folly embodies the way in which you can become receptive to the teacher of life. In terms of growth, failure and accomplishment are inseparable. It is all good and everything is leading you to participate with life more deeply.

The Master said: *"Great perfection will always appear chipped."* You cannot discover your capabilities if your idea of perfection makes you afraid to fail. A world perpetually evolving transcends the idea of imperfection. *Do not seek your idea of perfection; seek only authenticity.*

"One of little words has inner value." In the process of learning, you will find words are a measure of your inner certainty. When you feel the need to defend yourself, you are merely reassuring your own misgivings. Trusting in your power allows energy to mount without the use of words. *"Without looking out the window, you will discover the natural Way."* Everything you would want to experience *out there* must first be cultivated *in here.* This perspective enables you to have a stronger footing in the world around you.

"This is the inner strength that emerges from stillness." To find stillness, you must sometimes travel a *"journey of a thousand miles."* Eventually, you will discover that the power to succeed takes root beneath your feet. The actual journey has the dual effect of strengthening your inner direction, while fortifying your trust in the Way.

HSU Nourishing/Waiting

5th Degree: *Failure and success will test the depth and nature of your sincerity.*

"Too often man handles life as he does the bad weather;
he whiles away the time as he waits for it to stop."
– *Alfred Polgar*

"Waiting: If you are sincere, you have light and success." Hsu reveals the force of attraction that resonates from your beliefs. You are either nourishing a picture of success or failure, and the time of waiting will come to give form to both. The Master said: *"it furthers one to Cross the Great Water."* When you are fearless in testing the unknown, *"failure and success come to test the depth and nature of your sincerity."* It may seem like you are not moving forward when you are waiting, although life is testing your sincerity. If you are on the right course, this is a period of trial rather than defeat.

The Creative stirs below the Abysmal Water in the image of planting a field, while waiting for rain. It will come in its own time and impatience brings about nothing, although the time of waiting can be a time of cultivating.

Just as you test a rope by pulling on it, life is testing your sincerity against the tension of waiting. *When the world offers no response, you can hear the voice of your heart.* Life always seems to ask the same questions: "is it real…is *this* what you want?" If it is real, it will endure. Original sincerity binds you to your thread running through the way.

All that you experience reveals the thoughts you nourish. Hsu's message is that in the field of action, you generally find all that you are seeking.

You cannot interfere before the time is ripe, but if *"what you have planted is tended with sincerity, it will bear fruit. During the time of waiting, only the heart can reveal the answer."* You can only hear its voice when being forced to wait.

"The person who says it can't be done should not interrupt the person doing it." Most large corporations will expand during downturns in economic cycles and prove that growth is possible under any type of condition. *Waiting for rain* reflects your dependence upon natural cycles, although a commitment to growth can transform a down cycle into an opportunity for advancement.

In between the period of planting and harvesting, growth may not be apparent and yet, progress still occurs. A plant establishes a strong foundation of roots below the ground before it emerges from the earth. If its footing is shallow, it will not endure. This is how the time of waiting makes you stronger. *"Waiting means not advancing, yet, through progress the work is accomplished. Sincerity means the completion of the self and the Way is self-directing."* You find direction *within* only when it is lacking from without. Sincerity is the root that keeps you connected to the germinating power of life. *"When things are still small, you should not leave them without nourishment."* While you remain in a holding pattern, you imagine all sorts of scenarios. After a time of waiting only sincerity remains; if it is real, it will endure.

SUNG Conflict

6th Degree: *When you open, all obstacles will disappear.*

"Truth fears nothing but concealment."

– Chinese Proverb

"Heaven and water go their separate ways: The image of conflict." The profound and Abysmal Water move downward, while the Creative pushes upward and away in a situation of conflict and separation. Yet, in the Water, you can see yourself in life's *"mysterious mirror."* Life brings together similar things to separate productive energy from what has grown stagnant. Its creative and natural tension is always active, whether two highly charged individuals come together, or two unbalanced pressure systems collide. There will be change and there will be creative growth; it is simply nature's way.

"A cautious halt halfway brings success." When you meet life halfway, you open to what experience can teach you about yourself. People you meet are mirrors of how life brings you together propitiously. This is not a mystical event; life simply has a way of bringing like things together to balance and redistribute bound up energy. You are always exchanging energy with your environment, and as part of life's greater tapestry, you are subject to its economies.

The Master said: *"propitious meant you attract the things you need."* Like a trapped log in a river that encounters a spinning leaf, if two things are stuck and doing similar things, it is only a matter of time before they meet in the river of life. Believing in the idea of conflict is simply how you remain oblivious to how you may have become *stuck* and how you might let go.

Meeting contention in another, offers an opportunity that will teach you about your condition. *"When meeting another of contrary character, one would do well to examine themselves."* Difficulty *out there* seems to come out of nowhere, but nature shows us how the energy *released* was always *inherent* in the things that crashed together.

Without defensiveness, try owning the energy of a conflicted situation. Like nuclear fission, there is enormous energy released in the bonds that tie things together. Obstacles may block your progress, but they also present a tangible vehicle, which allows you to understand how you become stuck.

"When you open, all obstacles immediately disappear. When you learn not to contend with others, you no longer contend with the Way." Any barrier to your forward progress will always fill you with inner strength and clarity. As the image of pleading your case before an official, you can sometimes only understand what is important to you, when forced to defend it.

SHIH Collective Force

7th Degree: *To know fulfillment, you must nourish what is for the belly and not the eye.*

"If you don't stand for something, you will fall for anything."

–Chinese Proverb

"When there is conflict, individuals come together." The Abysmal Water stirs below the Receptive Earth, portraying how custom and duty can erode your sense of loyalty. Shih is a message about discovering value in what you do. As the image of many people gathering around a center, peer pressure can sometimes lead you away from your center. While it suggests the idea of serving, you can only serve others when you have turned inward to serve yourself.

Natural selection drives diversification and variety in all of life's creatures, and shows how individuation is an evolutionary mechanism. Beyond the flowery show that bears no fruit, *"it is the fruit and not the flower that sustains life."* The flower is attractive, but if you cut it for display, you will find no nourishment or fruit later, to sustain you. Do not trade your real nature because of the pressures of conformity.

The Master said, *"nourish what is for the belly and not the eye."* Shih reminds you to do what nourishes and does not deplete you. Whatever has left you feeling empty will lead you in the pursuit of instant gratification, as an endless cycle of fulfilling what is missing. When you find yourself drawn to this gratification process, you can be certain that something more fundamental remains unfulfilled.

The Profound Water brings you back to Earth to ask, *"Which is worth more, the person or the title?"* You can find pleasure in what you do only when it taps and authenticates your full capabilities. In the great field of action, you can become an instrumental part of the collective force only when you are fulfilled, and true to your nature.

PI Uniting

8th Degree: *When innate knowledge blends with the pathway, it will reveal your destiny.*

"We sleep, but the loom of life never stops and the pattern
which was weaving when the sun went down
is weaving when it comes up tomorrow."

– Henry Ward Beecher

"Holding together means uniting." Pi is an image of how the pathway reflects the well-being of your inner world. The Master said: *"when you are in a hurry, life moves quickly to slow you down; when you are angry, circumstances test your patience."* Since nature is on a mission to employ the best of what it might become, acknowledge how you too, are a part of this design. *"The way does not speak; it reveals by deeds and events."* Take time to observe how life is speaking to you to bring forward and define your individuality.

Stunted by the idea of *who* you should be, dreams become the messenger of a guiding source within. Harvesting these inner cues, you can begin to recognize how inspiration rises to offer meaning. Just as you evolve through actual experience and not by denying the world, you cannot deny or ignore inspiration rising within. *"Even in sleep, you continue your practice."*

When you are trapped in a transformative process, inspiration rises, whether through dreams, intuition or events to reveal the *way through.* Synchronicity is a word that describes this uniting process, where the inner and outer are drawn together. Inspiration can link an outward event that appears coincidental, with information that makes that event personally meaningful. As you connect inspiration to an outward event, you will find active intuition that validates your inner processes. This innate knowledge merges with the pathway to reveal your destiny.

Therapists explore dreams to uncover symbols that can re-empower a client in crisis. Pi is the image of someone walking, who suddenly stops to become observant. Bringing the inner and outer together, *ming* is a word that describes how the line separating the two is an illusion. Inspiration prods you along your path, while the pathway teaches you about your inner world. Without blending inner and outer clues, you may float aimlessly in the river of life. As the last of the section portraying the great *field of action,* ming is the unified awareness achieved when *me in here* and *that out there* have no separation.

"Everything is destiny; all things are already complete in oneself," you need only turn inward to bring your real nature forward.

SECTION TWO

Life's Rules of Engagement: Principles 9-16

"The Way is easy, yet people prefer by-paths."

HSIAO CH'U Small Restraint

9th Degree: *When obstacles appear insurmountable, you must only release the dam within.*

"The universe is full of magical things patiently waiting
for our wits to grow sharper."
– Eden Phillpotts

"Holding together, restraint is certain to come about." The Gentle Wind stirs above the Creative in the image of how the smallest effort makes creation possible. Hsiao Ch'u is the first principle that teaches you about *life's rules of* engagement and reveals how your power to create must come as a double-edged sword. On the one hand, the smallest effort will eventually bear fruit as the image of the fertile soil gathering in a river valley. It also suggests how the tiniest seed takes form in the ideas that you cultivate. The Master said: *"The Gentle has its own power, like water dripping onto stone."* All of experience is a reflection of your *constant determination.*

Hsiao Ch'u is a picture of how small things are domesticated and suggests how habitual responses are trained, and can lead to self-imposed restraint. If you chain a wild horse to a fence long enough, its spirit will not only be broken, it may also forget that it ever roamed free. The nuclear trigrams suggest *"dense clouds, no rain."* Condensation gathers energy above the Water, but the Winds of change cannot disperse it, and the atmosphere grows heavy and unproductive. Self-limiting ideas can take hold like a dam that blocks your forward progress.

Each time you discover meaning in life, you feel a sense of joy. Yet, joy is not something found on a distant horizon; meaning is always unfolding around you. Cultivating purity of thought will allow you to carry this joy of discovery with you, wherever you go.

When you lose your connection to life, you become trapped on the shores of a great river delta, which generates all thoughts into creation. As you participate with the forces of evolution, you will find that the quest requires little outward movement, only a change of perspective within.

You may be moving in circles, while obstacles appear to be everywhere. The smallest restraint can make you feel paralyzed, although when obstacles appear insurmountable, you must only release the dam within. Either take time to understand what you are creating or encounter it later, as an obstacle. To engage the energy of life, you must combine your power to create with the openness that makes anything possible.

LU Conduct/Treading

10th Degree: *Evolution requires you participate with life and not mystify it.*

"Use what talent you possess; the woods would be silent
if no birds sang except those that sang best."
– Henry Van Dyke

"Treading shows the basis of character; one who treads does not stay." One by-product of disowning your natural vitality is the way in which you create the idea of good and evil *out there* to avoid responsibility *in here.* Life always meets you half way, but as long as you are a victim, you will always see the world as a glass half-full. Filling the other portion of the glass is life's way of allowing you to discover your full capabilities.

The Joyous Lake is the daughter, reaching toward the Creative in the image of the weak treading on the power of the strong father. The exuberance of the child worries the father who looks upon his daughter with humor. Perhaps he finds humor in the innocent pursuit of something impossible to grasp. Of the energy of life, the Master said, *"Whoever lays hold of it will lose it."*

"The scriptures are the dim footprints of ancient kings. They tell us nothing of the force that guided their steps. Footprints are made by shoes, but they are far from being shoes." Lu asks you to focus on your footsteps because life will reveal itself differently in the unique pathway you walk on. Evolution requires that you participate with life and not

mystify it. *"The truth is not a sign that points to something beyond itself; it just is."* The truth you seek rests in every moment of your unfolding.

The word *destiny* derives from words that mean *to stand apart.* You cannot follow your destiny when you are following others. When you tread, you move within the course of events because *"that which treads does not stay."* Like a train that follows its own track, *"let your wheels move along old ruts."* You may embark on a similar journey, but your destination will always be different.

Lu asks you to find a personal relationship to what you hold to be sacred. Vague taboos that arise from ambiguous boundaries, which only repress your natural vitality, can sometimes lead you away from wellness. *"Treading on the tail of the tiger,"* you are naturally endowed with aggression, driven to survival with a primitive urge *to hunt.* You may track the footprints of a greater power in each experience, but you can never truly capture it. You can only harness your carriage to its wonders and follow joyfully.

When dogma takes the place of actual experience, it shackles you to *"lectures that are no better than footprints in the dust."* Yet, of the evolutionary power of life, *"go up to it and you will not see its head; follow behind and you will not see its rear. Treading on the tail of the tiger, it does not bite."* It does not bite because you follow behind.

When you have lost interest in the mystery of life, Lu becomes a shining light upon your footsteps. To give this power name or form, you can only lose it.

T'AI Peace

11th Degree: *Being free of desires, you will discover that the empire is at peace of its own accord.*

"If I keep a green bough in my heart, the singing bird will come."

– Chinese Proverb

"Good conduct, then contentment; thus calm prevails in the image of peace." T'ai is the image of moving harmoniously with the flow of events to discover the peace that comes when you are content to follow. *"All weak elements are forced to take their departure when the two great forces of Yin and Yang come together."* Just as Yin and Yang move in turn, where one moves *"upward, while the other moves downward,"* one aspect of life leads us forward, while another moves downward to eliminate the unnecessary. In either case, what emerges is the *"unobstructed and harmonious union that comes to eliminate all weakness."*

In life's relentless pursuit of a better way, anything that would block its forward progress must pass. Perhaps that was why Tao was said to *"treat the creatures like straw dogs."* What is tightly held in your arms will leave you unable to embrace life's gifts. You are merely borrowing all you hold and might as well let it pass freely from your grasp.

Life pulls you toward the path of productive growth that will always be the path of least resistance *out there*. You may not see it that way however, because you confuse fear *in here* with resistance perceived to be *out there*. By reinforcing this illusion, fear keeps you trapped in your growth. The proof comes anytime you knock on the door of fear: *it always opens.* When it opens, enormous energy is released, which can be very exhilarating.

Being free of judgment and clinging to nothing, you will discover a pathway of peace. "*If you keep a green bough in your heart, the singing bird will come.*" This joy of spirit roosts when you practice *the art of living.*

Peace comes from knowing that tomorrow will take care of itself because yesterday was meaningful. This allows you to be present and observant now. The Master said: "*be in awe of timelessness. This is how you can dwell in timelessness. If I cease from desire and remain still, the empire will be at peace of its own accord.*" Nothing of value can be threatened because if it is meaningful, it will remain. What is relegated to the past, were those things that were unnecessary. Representing your evolutionary journey, T'ai is the image of a person flowing in the great river of life.

Trusting in the Way joyfully, it moves you forward, without the need to shake you from your self-imposed obstructions. "*Make your home the inevitable, then grief and the pursuit of joy cannot intrude. There is no folly greater than having too many desires.*" Each day, the mysterious carriage appears. "*The clouds are the carriage and the sun and the moon are the steeds.*" Embarking upon each new day with a sense of discovery, you can move joyfully to receive the gifts that each unfolding moment brings to you.

P'I Standstill

12th Degree: *Contentment cannot be held in the hand, but lives perpetually in your heart.*

"Fresh activity is the only means of overcoming adversity."

– Goethe

"Things do not stay forever united and can lead to standstill." The danger of Peace is that it can lead to progressive stagnation. This is because of the lack of *necessary tension* that life uses to generate novelty. In other words, too much of a good thing can unwittingly lull you to sleep in the arms of stagnation. P'i suggests the things you hold that keep you from moving forward.

Observing nature, you will see that nothing comes to a standstill. A pool of water that has separated from the rivers and sea will eventually stagnate or dry up. The nuclear trigram of the Mountain is immovable, while the Gentle Wind encourages movement. *Together, they ask you to release your expectations, so that you can discover the joy of following life on its terms.* Do not root yourself in the momentary thing that made you happy because contentment is simply the proper response in following. If you do not expect anything, you can discover the magic that life has in store for you.

Exploring what it means to follow, the Master said: *"contentment cannot be held in the hand, although it can live perpetually in the heart."* You can plant something in a pot and fill it with water, but if it is not provided proper drainage, it will die.

As a lesson about letting go, P'i suggests how desiring not to remain full allows you to be filled anew.

In Youthful Folly, movement allowed you to gain the same wisdom that can arise without going anywhere. During the Time of Waiting, the voice of the heart emerged. Sincerity negotiates with the obstacle, *"do I really want this enough to wait?"* Once you made the commitment to persevere, you pleaded your case before an official and came to terms with something so important you had to defend it. Trusting in the *Way,* the empire is at peace of its own accord, whether you choose to worry about it, or not. If you find that you are not moving forward, you will discover that it is *your will* and not the Way.

As an image of the mouth, and the symbol for "not," it suggests how *"standstill is giving way."* You can let go, or find that something more profound will come to help you give way. To follow the easier path, try releasing your attachment to a specific outcome. You will find that you were blocking a greater movement that left you unable to receive life's greater gifts.

TUNG JEN Fellowship

13th Degree: *If you understand nature's symmetries, you will use no counting rods.*

"Humankind has not woven the web of life.

We are but one thread within it.

Whatever we do to the web, we do to ourselves."

– *Chief Seattle*

"Heaven together with fire: the image of fellowship." The Clinging Flame mimics the fire of the Creative above, like stars that sparkle to reflect cosmic time and order. Tung Jen is a message that asks you to overcome your sense of feeling separate from everything around you. Transcending your illusion of boundaries, you can begin to see the part you play in the greater movement of life.

Everything in the universe is interacting and exchanging energy in some way and although you cannot see nature's symmetries and connectivity, they are there. *"One who understands the activities of Nature, uses no counting rods."* All things are equal in the eyes of nature because *"all things mutually involve each other."* You can only understand the essence of *one thing* by observing everything that stands next to, and influences it.

Let go of any limitations and boundaries that hold you back from seeing this essential unity. The Master said: *"Blending the disparities of ten thousand years into complete purity, all things mutually involve each other."* When we look backward, we see meaning. Why would the same not hold true for the future? You will find that both are changed when you opening to the perpetual moment.

The primary trigrams suggest an atmosphere of organization and distinction, while the nuclear trigrams portray life's interconnectivity and impartiality. The ancients found a predictable way of marking time by observing the planets moving through constellations in a fixed rhythm. Observing these cycles provided the knowledge of when to plant and harvest, allowing civilization to thrive. While these patterns revealed how what is above affects what is below, it also showed the outline or behavior of a larger organism.

All people are complex networks of cells, but we only recognize them in one form. Your perception makes distinctions in the natural world that are not necessarily there. If you could see life from nature's perspective, you would see all lines fading into one giant organism of sustenance and movement. Being impartial will bring added power to everything you do.

As a reproduction of a larger organism, your body is like the environment. In similar proportion to the earth, you are made of 23% carbon, 1.4% calcium, 2.6% nitrogen, 1.1% phosphorous and 71% water. It is no mystery that you share common properties with everything around you, since all plants and animals descended from an ancestor, three billion years old. Tung Jen reminds you of life's interconnectivity and asks you to experience how you are connected to all you see.

The Master said: *"should you act from knowledge of the constant, your actions will lead to impartiality. The hundred bones, the nine cavities and the six organs: which one shall I love best?"* Just as you care for your entire body without making distinctions, do not draw lines that separate you from the web of life.

Tung Jen is the image of quietly knowing without being able to describe it. When you give and receive through others, you are able to move beyond your self-limiting structures and orientation to life. *"Life becomes brilliant when purpose shines its light upon it."* You are not made meaningless and irrelevant. On the contrary, you are awakened to greater meaning and purpose.

TA YU Possession in Great Measure

14th Degree: *If you are not playing the host, you will discover that you are the guest.*

"In the depth of winter, I finally learned
that there was in me, an invincible summer."
-- Albert Camus

"The character is firm, strong, ordered and clear: the image of possession in great measure." Ta Yu is the image of life's inexhaustible energy source that is available when you open yourself to nature's drive toward excellence. As you explore the ways in which you exercise control, observe how life comes to release you. The Master said: *"Do not play the host, but become the guest."* If you can transcend your need for control, you can become the recipient of the subtle treasures that life has in store for you.

In the natural world, we are the only creatures who attempt to play the host, rather than being the guest. We have become so disconnected from knowing what it is like to hunt for our nourishment that we behave less like animals and more like trees. You might argue that unlike trees, you can move freely about. Yet, you come and go to the same places each day, drawing sustenance from a refrigerator. Even while you barely look over your dashboard, desktop and television, life still finds productive ways of leading you forward. When you open to life's power for potential, you can possess its energy in greater measure.

A tree provides shelter to the tiny nests hidden within its branches, but it does not play the host because it opens itself to the wind, rain and the tiny insects that nourish and steward its pollination and rebirth. The wind and the rain are not the host because they are generated by the changing pressure systems in the atmosphere. The earth is not the host because it responds to these atmospheric changes, and the moon makes its great bodies of water rise and fall. If the oldest things in the universe are not in control, then why do you attempt to play the host?

Playing the host without understanding the host is how you unwittingly create your own misfortune. When you learn to become the guest of a greater unfolding, you can flow into life's purposeful movement toward the best of what it might become.

"Once there was a seabird, which was blown onto land. A kind prince ordered a solemn reception, where he offered it wine and invited the townspeople to share in the celebration. He ordered musicians to play their best

compositions and slaughtered cattle to feed the winged visitor. Confused to see human faces and dazed by the symphonies, the unhappy seabird died of despair." Your attempts to play the host may be well meaning, but you are limited in understanding of how the way moves. It is better to remain the guest when moving within a larger dwelling because you are ignorant to the ways of the host.

Trusting that something more profound might understand your needs in ways that you cannot, *"all things in the universe have a purpose; is it right that you should be different?"* The only reason the future remains a mystery is because life has a special predisposition for exploring possibilities. Through its dance of randomness, it generates innovation and novelty. When you are not busy organizing your life, you will discover that you are the guest of something that demonstrates a greater purpose in leading you.

Ta Yu is the image of a hand opening to present an offering. Because the hand is open, it is now able to receive. The greatest teacher learns by teaching, and the most celebrated artists allow their work to lead them. Similarly, if you trust in the energy of life to lead you forward, you can access power or inspiration in greater measure.

CH'IEN Moderation

15th Degree: *If you know no boundaries, you will discover no limitations.*

"One who rides a tiger is afraid to dismount."

– Chinese Proverb

"One who possesses something great should not make it too full." The Mountain bows down to the Receptive Earth in an unusual display of modesty and temperance. Even the summit of Mount Everest contains proof of its humble beginnings, in rocks that were once formed in a shallow sea.

"The vessel in the temple of Chou stood upright when empty, but overturned when full. Rather than fill it to the brim, it is better to have stopped in time," so nothing gets overturned. Ch'ien offers a message about turning back and ceasing action to ensure nothing comes to undo the things that can lead to excess.

Humility is a necessary virtue that reveals the fine line between taking and giving. In our effort to grow abundant produce, we apply chemicals that ward off disease, although they destroy the bees and ladybugs that keep the plants healthy. Tourists are attracted to colorful reefs where they can snorkel with abundant fish populations. As hotels appear along the coastline, they tear out the mangroves that trap and process excess nutrients and pollutants in the water. As the water quality in the coral reef environment diminishes, the reefs perish, and all that the tourists came to see is destroyed.

As nature moves to purify itself, we discover that what we throw away does not necessarily go away. Because you cannot trace the line of excess, *"it is better to have stopped in time."* In all you eat and do, strike a balance between productive Yang and replenishing Yin.

Life is an interconnected system of symbiotic processes where one species cannot be viewed as being more important than the other. Even while viruses and diseases reveal molecular struggles that might conflict with the well-being of the host, evolution requires these same mutations and deviations, which lead species to survive and adapt.

At the same time that developers are destroying the mangroves, many of our important medications are farmed from marine organisms that thrive on the reef. Moderation suggests that *"turning back is how the Way moves."* Turning back to re-explore the enormous power of natural processes, municipalities now recognize the long-term value of preserving natural watersheds, when compared to the cost of building expensive water treatment facilities. When you turn back, you allow nature to do what it has done perfectly since the beginning of time.

"The way that leads forward seems to lead backward." This perpetual cycle appears in economics and in nature. After every rise, you may fall, but you only appear to be rising and falling in relation to your expectations. In the larger scheme of things, all things continue to move forward. Progress is usually a product of hindsight.

Imagine an airplane encircling the earth. At some point, it would appear to be turning back, although the pilot and passengers would disagree. All of this activity is indiscernible from your limited perspective. The Master said: *"what is vast resembles nothing because if it resembled anything, it would become small."* Nature turns back, while still moving forward when the seasons change.

Turning back, you can find contentment in modesty; through modesty, you will re-connect with the way. Do not become so distant from your actions that you forget you are a part of both the *smallness* and *largeness* of life. *"There are times when you climb and times when you fall. The climb is difficult, but the fall is quick and inexorable."* As you rise, you can offset your times of falling with the knowledge of this turning.

Moderation ensures you do not close your mind with structures and ideas that can become obstructions. In your search for absolutes, you must succumb to the gravity of the unknowable.

"When there is nothing that you cannot overcome, no one knows the limit." When there is something you must overcome, *you discover your limits.* Ch'ien suggests that if you are content to know no boundaries, you will discover no limitations. As the image of establishing limits on the outer world through words and ideas, it asks you to turn back and be content not to know.

"The Way goes round and round. Being great, it is described as receding. Receding, it is described as far away. Being far away, it is described as turning back." In the Great Circle, turning back is how all things continue in their forward movement.

YU Enthusiasm

16th Degree: *If you make your home in the inevitable, you will arrive exactly where you need to be.*

> *"Chance is always powerful. Let your hook always be cast;*
> *In the pool where you least expect it, there will be a fish."*
> *– Ovid*

"One who possesses something great and is modest is sure to have enthusiasm." Yu is the image of a child riding an elephant where spontaneous enthusiasm, combined with nature's enormous transformative power will allow you to trample any barriers that would impede your forward progress. Like the athlete who enters the *zone,* by overcoming resistance, movement is effortless, and you feel as if you can accomplish anything. Yet, nothing in the environment has really changed, although somewhere *within,* the illusion of resistance dissipates. Enthusiasm is your devotion to moving forward when you tap life's positive and free flowing energy in this way.

Atoms within matter are mostly composed of empty space. Yet, at the center is a positively charged core, which accounts for 99.95% of the atom's mass or energy. This positively charged core has the effect of drawing electrons into orbit. One atom builds upon another, forming molecules, until you walk into a room to create a presence that others cannot fail to recognize. Yet, most of who you are remains empty space, energized by moving fields. The Master said: *"the power of becoming resides in a positively charged core."* You can approach life with a positive attitude, or you can resist and fight against it. The Way is much easier when you follow the path of least resistance.

"When you make your home in the inevitable, you will arrive exactly where we need to be." Banging endlessly against a closed door, you might discover that the entire time, another door remained open. This is the sublimity you will discover when following life. The nuclear trigram of the Abysmal Water suggests a wellspring coming up against the Mountain of a closed door. Water cannot flow up the hill of a hardened perspective, but a profound inner shifting can open the doors of inertia when devotion to movement magnetizes opportunity.

The door was always open; it is a shift in awareness that allows you to find it. Like the athlete who enters the zone, your devotion to movement reveals how the *wall* is always an illusion. It is your dedication to moving forward that will ensure your success.

SECTION THREE

Promotion and Advancement: Principles 17-24

"Great fullness seems empty, yet use will not drain."

SUI Following

17th Degree: *If you return from the darkness with gold, others will naturally follow.*

"We can easily forgive a child who is afraid of the dark;
the real tragedy of life is when men are afraid of the light."
– Plato

"Where there is enthusiasm, there is sure to be a following." If you use nature as a role model for leadership, you can effectively lead others by modeling its ways. The sage who had become Master of the self and the pathway was encouraged to develop *"harmony in one's larger relationship to life."* Transcending your personal journey, even while you lead others, you remain a student of the germinating power of life.

The Arousing Thunder rests within the middle of the Joyous Lake, representing a calm withdrawal and the image of delegation. When winter gave way to spring, lightning was believed to withdraw into the earth to regenerate the unseen seeds below. In the image of withdrawal and retreat, it is time to cultivate the unseen talents of those below. Empowering those you lead, you can nurture each individual to build the strength of the group. Sui is the image of how footsteps naturally follow each other.

The Master said: *"If you are a model to the empire, then the constant virtue will not be wanting. To benefit others without extracting gratitude, and to steward without exercising authority is virtue."* Sensing the appropriate time when things are in their proper place, you may leave what you have built in the hands of those who follow.

"Desiring to lead the people, one must, in one's person, follow behind them. One takes the place ahead of the people, yet causes no obstruction. That is why the empire supports the leader joyfully and never tires of doing so." Firm like a Mountain, you can inspire and not impede. Gentle like the Wind, you can bring projects to completion by trusting others to carry forward your vision.

As a leader, you can operate from insecurity, threatened by the strengths of others or, you can cultivate the talents of those who follow in a way that you are lifted to a higher level. You are made stronger and will achieve greater success only when you learn to delegate. The empire or enterprise will only support the leader who nurtures others in this way. You can take your place ahead without causing any obstruction behind.

Observing how nature returns in predictable cycles, all enterprises will require stages of completion and renewal. You can *"hammer something to a point, yet the sharpness cannot be preserved forever."* When communication is clear and expectations are understood, productivity thrives on results alone. Those who follow must know *ownership* to experience *accomplishment.* Nature serves its creatures by rewarding productive results not weakness.

Putting vision and accomplishment in the hands of those you lead ensures integrity in the enterprise. To lead in a way others follow joyfully, is the sign of true leadership. *"When the task is finished and the work done, the people all say, 'it happened to us naturally.'"* A leader, guided by the laws of nature, will not be worn down by failing to rely on the strengths of others.

KU Decay

18th Degree: *All things are supple when alive, but become hard when dead.*

"The real voyage of discovery consists not
in seeking new landscapes, but in having new eyes."

– Marcel Proust

"Work on what has spoiled; afterwards there is order." Routine can take on a life of its own and over time, all things require renewal. Following the way of nature, work on what has been spoiled by decay to foster a rebirth and to bring vitality to what is old and outworn. Ku portrays how being placed in a yielding position to nourish others can sometimes turn the Wind into the image of drifting. Failing to recognize the necessary cycles of completion and renewal, a situation can move steadily toward a state of stagnation.

The Master said: *"all things in nature are supple when alive and hard when dead."* A business environment, being comprised of individuals must also be established on a foundation of individual growth to keep the enterprise alive. Observing what can lead the situation to become hard and dead, prune away what will prevent forward progress.

Some leaders define their worth by solving the problems of others, and those who follow look to them as a problem solver. You can sometimes lose your vision of the larger picture by tending to its many parts. Regardless of the reason, growth can lose its suppleness.

"The Mountain is the beginning and end." It is associated with autumn when the height of creation ends and begins anew. In the image of seeds falling to the ground, harvest the seeds of the future by removing the outer husk or protective covering of the past. To work on what has spoiled, separate what is dead from what will bring new life.

"You observe life's power in what you can see and hear. Its potential remains in the unknown and mysterious." Crossing the Great Water to observe the situation with a fresh perspective, success is assured through systematic renewal. Stagnation only exists while you avoid the inevitable death of the old way. To tap the potential of something, you must come to terms with what must pass.

"Before the starting point, three days. After the starting point, three days." Three months of spring follow three months of winter to bring about growth, but only because three months of autumn ushered in decline. With nature as your teacher, you will be undaunted by the

changing climate, and merely set upon the task of reinvigorating renewal. You may not immediately see the cause of decay, although you can observe the lack of vitality or hardness surrounding the situation. The new beginning cannot manifest until you are willing to allow the ending to come.

LIN Approach

19th Degree: *When you place yourself in a position to help another, you will discover your real capabilities.*

"In creating, the only hard thing is to begin:

a grass blade's no easier to make than an oak."

– James Lowell

"When there are things to be done, one becomes great." Approach describes the work that you can do that will make you great. You receive a new job or promotion because you have delegated in a way that leaves you open to greater opportunity. If you place yourself in a position to help another, you will discover your real capabilities.

At times, nature advances by breaking through. You can also heighten productivity by breaking through the *difficult* to discover the *easy*. Approach embodies why life only meets you half way: *the other half allows you to discover your capabilities.* As a leader, you may know the destination, but those who follow must discover their own way.

When achievement rests upon the shoulder of the individual, through systems that both ensure and reward growth, you set a course for success that has the momentum of a wheel in motion. It is put in continual motion by the enthusiasm that comes from an unfettered structure focused on growth.

"The firm penetrates and grows; great success through correctness." Being firm in helping others grow, you must sometimes approach the difficult task of breaking through their walls. With nature as your teacher, you will see that it is no different from how life leads you; life is always breaking down your walls to unleash the best of what you can be. Approaching the difficult clears the air. Honesty always transforms the difficult into the easy.

"The Earth above the Lake; the image of approach." Lin is the image of making contact and is associated with a willingness to serve. You can only serve others if you are steadfast in helping them grow. *"The sage is inexhaustible in the will to teach without limits."* When you make contact, you create a truth environment where growth occurs exponentially. Anytime you find yourself working in an environment where truth and growth are non-existent, the lack of integrity undermines productivity in a way that makes going to work a chore in, and of itself.

Inspired by nature, allow those you lead to bring forward their own vision. Holding to a vision of where you are going, you must also foster *ownership* in those who follow. When subordinates can create their own vision, and identify a sense of owning the outcome, the enterprise achieves a sense of fullness, of which *"use will not drain."*

KUAN Contemplation

20th Degree: *You can only lead others toward growth if you are willing to grow yourself.*

"Life can only be understood backwards but it must be lived forwards."

– Kierkegaard

"The wind blows over the earth: the image of contemplation." You have the opportunity to climb the heights of a tower you have built to obtain a wider view. The bird's eye view offered by this tower suggests finding the white space that will allow you to remain objective. In this way, you establish a course for the future by reinvigorating your roots.

Whenever the Wind blows over the Earth, it ushers in a changing climate. The most common celebrations of ancient times revolved around the harvest festivals of autumn. Perhaps this was because of the fear and reverence they felt as the days grew darker, and the natural world began to die away. It was an important time however, because what was done in earnest during this time, laid the seeds for a springtime to come. This is the meaning of contemplation: take inventory of the past and reinvigorate the seeds of the future.

Wind suggests purity and the washing of the hands. The Master said: *"the ablution has been made, but not yet, the offering."* The "ablution" or washing of the hands is how you *"remove the residue of red dust,"* or the hardened perspective that can accumulate on your journey. The "offering" is your willingness to remain malleable in all you do.

"The sage understands the way forward by observing the cycles that endure. If you don't believe, just look at September, look at October!" When you look backward, you will see many cycles that remain constant, although you barely remember the vague situations that become meaningless over time. By recognizing all that is transient, you can observe the *carved block*. Once experience assumes a specific shape, it is time to let it go.

Hold only to that which cultivates growth. In each situation, *"retain the lesson but not the carved block."* Other than its transitory manifestations, *"the great image has no shape."*

The *"thread running through the Way"* becomes your footsteps through the path of change. Your destiny is revealed by that part of you that remains unchanged against the wheel of changing events. *"Returning to one's roots is known as stillness. This is what is meant by returning to one's destiny."* You can move through the changes without being pulled from your center. Although you walk less, you discover more. The core of who you are only sharpens against the vicissitudes of experience.

The Master said: *"When one is at ease with themselves, one is near Nature. This is to let Nature take its own course."* When you are just so, you are not defending anything. *"When 'this' and 'that' have no opposites, you discover life's very axis."*

Contemplation allows you to see that all things are equal: the good and bad, the difficult and easy are merely the ebbing and flowing face of change.

"When a leader is right with themselves, things will get done without giving orders. When they are not right with themselves, they may give orders, but they will not be obeyed." You can only lead others toward growth if you are willing to grow yourself.

To others, your humility makes you the representation of *"how great fullness seems empty. Full of trust, they look up to view the divine Way where the four seasons do not deviate."* In contemplating, *"you partly give and partly take."* You take time for yourself and reinvigorate your roots, but you also become *"something for the world to view. The more one gives, the more one comes to possess."*

A student asked: *"Sir, how is it that you are old, but have the appearance of a child?"* The Master replied: *"It is because I have not been worn down by going against the Way."*

SHIH HO Biting Through

21st Degree: *To keep others down, you would have to live your life on your knees.*

"Honest differences are often a sign of progress."

– Mahatma Gandhi

"There is something between the corners of the mouth: the image of biting through." Supervisors need subordinates to maintain their leadership position, and subordinates are always striving to climb higher. *"The high and low incline toward each other"* each time varying pressure systems collide, or when lightning crosses the expanse of sky

to ground itself in the earth. Whether something is hot, cold, high, low, empty or full, energy is exchanged as life pursues balance. As a leader, you can emulate how nature finds harmony, even while it honors differences. Real success should be a win/win situation for all. Apparent differences merely lay the path for change.

The Master said: *"when the firm and yielding are distinct from each other, when the high and low move separately; when anything reaches its extreme, it must turn back."* Unlike Thunder, which always follows Lightning, the Fire is yielding to the Arousing Thunder and the disturbance suggests a need for necessary balance. Something *"is not in its appropriate place"* and justice or balance must be re-established.

Your idea of justice may not resemble justice in the natural world. *"The high it brings down, the low it lifts up; It takes from what is in excess, in order to make good of what is deficient."* Justice in nature is how the high is brought low, so the low can be lifted up. Life does not demonstrate retribution; it merely seeks improvement. Biting through is a foundation of impartiality that allows all things to flourish.

"When two sides raise arms against each other, it is the one that is sorrow-stricken that wins." The voice of the oppressed can be woeful as they lose a sense of the value of living. We see how their voices are heard through violent acts of frustration. Nature is a profound teacher in the way all things remain equal, *although they are not the same.* When opposition emerges, change has already begun. It is better to follow where the changes might lead you.

"There is something between the corners of the mouth." Shih Ho is the image of teeth biting through obstruction to communication. You

can wear yourself out trying to make things equal if you do not recognize that they *are* equal. Biting through is a way of discovering *"the ten thousand things may be one, yet they diverge in nature as they issue forth."*

"Leveling out is going two ways at once." Going two ways at once must be a win/win situation. *"Favor, when it is bestowed on an individual comes to startle as much as when it is withdrawn."* It is better to reward *results* than to bestow favoritism, so that those who follow discover an *equal opportunity* for success.

A free economy is one example of how the *natural way* is not always the *obvious way*. It works because it allows *what is* to take its own course, unimpeded by unnatural restrictions. At the heart of the difficulty, the solution has already begun to manifest itself. You can know the outcome by blending differences into something new.

All things are equal in the eyes of nature; equality is a level playing field for life's diverse creatures. It is unnatural to think *one* way is the *only* way. The Master said: *"the owl can catch fleas at night but cannot see a mountain during the day. This is because different things have different natures."* Do not measure those who follow with a common denominator. Nature teaches that biting through is life's freedom to become.

PI Grace

22nd Degree: *When you become lost, life always hands you a map that says: you are here.*

"If a man carefully examines his thoughts he will be surprised to find how much he lives in the future. His well being is always ahead."

—Emerson

"Fire at the foot of the Mountain: the image of grace." Seasons can change gracefully or destructively. Either way, nature's behavior cannot be classified in terms of good and bad. We build homes in what was once a desert, irrigate our gardens during times of drought, and wonder why the trees in the hillside catch on fire.

The earth builds mountains and islands by shifting its tectonic plates. It paves the way for renewal through fire, floods and landslides. We stand within a sliver of time in geological terms, and erect structures on an ever-changing landscape. Since the beginning of its existence, the earth has always been very much alive. Pi is a message about making peace with the changes: *"who knows what is good and what is bad?"*

In the image of how things are valued, the Master said: *"the Way is benevolent and excels on bestowing."* Nature accomplishes new growth by removing old growth, although you may sometimes put labels of value on every experience. Rooted in judgment, you sometimes cannot see how *"good fortune perches on apparent disaster."*

Obstruction *in here* is often overcome through the breaking down of what you cling to *out there.* Over time, you will recognize all experience as the graceful way life takes the lead to coach you toward renewal. Pi is translated to mean *because;* and suggests that life does not happen to you, it happens *because* of you.

"One, who is open to the Way, will gladly embrace it. One, who is not open to it and told about it, will laugh out loud at it." Similarly, one who is crying, might not realize how life nourishes the unseen garden within. Something has yet to grow and in this case, awareness must evolve before value can be found in the experience.

"Once a farmer's mare ran away. Afterward, his neighbor came by to console him. The farmer said, "Who knows what is good and what is bad?" The next day the mare returned with a stallion and the neighbor congratulated him. The farmer responded, "Who knows what is good and what is bad?" The following day the farmer's son was thrown from the stallion and broke his leg and again the neighbor consoled him. "Who knows what is good and what is bad," said the farmer. Within the same week, the army came to conscript the farmer's son, who was dismissed because of his broken leg. The neighbor finally agreed, "Who knows what is good and what is bad?"

The Mountain has a Fire within it, like a volcano where pressure accumulates and demands release. You can emulate grace and open joyfully, or you will find that events will force this energy out of hiding. Whenever you become lost, life brings you home. Forced to sit still while you discover meaning in what unfolds, you can imagine life whispers, "welcome back."

Grace works to soften the vicissitudes of your emotional states. As you grow older, experience softens the sharp edges until all that remains is the light of understanding, which grows within. The light shining from your eyes commemorates your journey of a thousand miles. No matter the trial, everything always worked out.

The monuments you build to commemorate the past can become prisons. In proportion to your unwillingness to leave them, you will experience the power of grace. If you measure the vicissitudes of life, all things become equal over time. Grace is a message of optimism without judgment: *who knows what is good and what is bad.* On the pathway, you will discover *Nothing Bad Happens in Life.* By understanding the way of grace, you have the opportunity to stand as a model of grace to others.

Emulating the graceful way nature achieves renewal, you can be steadfast in revealing the way of grace to others. You cannot cover and protect those who follow from a natural pathway of growth. You can however, be the Light that shines upon their footsteps. When you measure the vicissitudes of life, all things become equal. To lead with grace, strive to uncover the value hidden in every challenge.

PO Splitting Apart

23rd Degree: *All of life will not change you; it unfolds as a way to unmask you.*

"Life is a quarry, out of which we are to mold
chisel and complete a character."
– Goethe

"The Mountain emerges on the Earth: the image of splitting apart." The Mountain achieves its great height by its willingness to be lifted by the moving landscape. Remaining firm like a Mountain, you must be Receptive to what leads you forward. It reflects how feelings must break through any firm ideas rooted above. Nature does not remain stagnant and brings rain after a time of oppressive heat. Like emotions, weather is the changing expression of the atmosphere.

You cannot remain unyielding in the ideas that detach you from your feelings, and Po captures the image of how the heart moves differently from the mind. In the image of carving, pruning or being split apart, life does not change you; it simply carves away the layers that will unmask your real nature. Like fruit that has fallen to the earth, the seed can only take root once the protective covering disintegrates.

While you may understand that change must come, you may cling to the illusion of what you need. During the time of splitting apart, you will discover new life stirring beneath the mind's abstractions. The Master said: *"danger and delight grow on one stalk"* and necessity, as the power of circumstances, leads you to adapt to a changing climate.

Sincerity and authenticity are necessary virtues of good leadership and are cultivated by feelings and not the mind. *Sensitivity* makes you receptive to the nuances of transformation and Po represents your willingness to remain *compassionate* in all you do. Feelings make all experiences valuable. Without feelings you will be forced to *turn back* to discover compassion.

The ancient text seems to suggest that somehow, our normal perspective has everything backwards. Conflict makes us defensive but it comes to break our protective covering; the unnecessary blockages we create will merely evaporate when we become open. You may defend your concrete perspective when approaching others; even while they have come to help you let it go. All of experience presents you with a mysterious mirror that reflects the well-being of your inner world.

"When graced with understanding, success can exhaust itself in the image of splitting apart. Those above can assure their position by giving generously to those below." A business, being comprised of individuals, will suffocate beneath the layers of red tape. You can establish a system of numbers for those who follow, but without sensitivity, you cannot truly lead them. Emulating the nature, give generously to those below just as *"the high it presses down; the low it lifts up."*

Following life is a profound exercise in learning to overturn your mindset. The idea of Splitting Apart removes the protective covering of the past so you may grow to meet the future. The same hand forced open to give is now open to receive.

FU Return

24th Degree: *Progress for the leader is marked by a slow return to original sincerity.*

'Sow a thought, reap an action; sow an action, reap a habit.
Sow a habit, reap a character; sow a character, reap a destiny."

– Proverb

"Thunder within the earth: the image of a turning point." The Arousing Thunder stirs the Receptive Earth and represents a turning point or a time for return. In virtually all cultures, solar rituals were performed during the winter solstice when the sun was believed to be reborn. As the days commenced to grow longer in the West, the ancients burned Yule logs and decorated world trees. Using celestial orbs, they celebrated the birth of the sun's return.

In the East, *"the kings of antiquity closed the passes during the winter solstice."* The birth of the new sun embodied Yang's return to the earth and because it was new, it was weak and required nurturing. By closing the passes, people stayed indoors and businesses came to a halt, while the empire focused on nurturing the power of the newborn Yang.

In ancient times, we celebrated the return of the sun during the winter solstice at the end of December. It is interesting that this coincides with the celebration of a returning *son,* as if an ancient rumor may have evolved differently. People wait for this return because they believe that the world is fundamentally *bad* when it is actually very *good.*

Before and after always follow each other, but doors must close before new doors can open. In Fu, you return to close the door and find a new one opening: one that reveals life's fundamental goodness.

As the image of moving in the opposite direction or retracing a path, you can find closure by understanding the cycle of cause and effect. Closing will always generate events that return you to become more open.

The Master said: *"When one does nothing at all, nothing is undone."* Although you may not appear to be moving forward, *"progress is often marked by a slow return to original sincerity."* The original sincerity that makes others follow a leader is often lost in the details that set out to describe it. As a leader, you must stay connected to the sincerity of why you lead others. If it is real, it will endure. A return to sincerity means that nothing will ever need to be *undone.*

"Return shows the stem of character." The same issues you faced in the beginning always seem to crop up. Your beliefs will always fight against the forces of life that would keep you open. What you defend as absolute will threaten others in a way that leads them to defend their beliefs even more. Taking personal responsibility for the part you play in stalking adversity, you can discern the thread from the beginning to recognize how we create our own misfortune. The stem of character may be firm but it thrives on the nourishing power of change.

When you own your condition, constant rejection reflects your inability to commit. Obstruction *out there* always reveals the closed door *in here*. If you are contemplating leaving, everything seems to validate why you should go. Yet, you are creating this very experience to validate what you already believe.

Adversity has a way of shaving away beliefs that no longer serve you. Let them go. Return to sincerity so that others will follow you joyfully. *"Composure straightens out one's inner life; righteousness will square one's external life."* Your world will be different only when you take active responsibility for making it better. At the core of Return, is the sense of returning to the beginning of a cycle.

By mastering the self, the *Way,* and after being a leader in orchestrating *"harmony in one's larger relationship to life,"* the sage moved deeper along the pathway of initiation. The Master said: *'The sage understands the future by revisiting the past. Knowing that which is to come requires backward movement."*

We return to the teachings of the great Masters who developed this philosophy of nature as a pathway to success and wellness.

The Great Masters

Taoist philosophy captures an appreciation for the seamless unity of life, without losing a sense of self. This emphasis on individual empowerment makes Taoism different from many Eastern philosophies.

At the same time, life is not viewed as a collection of independent things, but instead, as an endless flow of interaction. Any order observed is simply the momentary and organic field of relationships called *Tao*. We take our place in the whole by being the unique creature nature designed us to be.

The philosophers of ancient China used the principles of nature to promote an understanding of how rulers and their people could practice its ways. The Legalists initiated a movement toward reform, and sought to change ritual observances into laws. In the middle of the sixth century BC, the most famous of Chinese thinkers, K'ung fu-tzu, known as Confucius, led a group of followers to oppose the Legalist's efforts, which he believed ignored man's moral nature.

By the age of twenty-five, Confucius had organized a preparatory school and had performed duties in local government, where he tested his theories in public office. At some point however, he went into exile. While he is celebrated as a national hero, he died believing he was a failure.

Exploring the ideas of more ancient times, he reintroduced the concept of *Tao.* He described it as the active principle that was more apparent when people knew their place within society. Concerned with practical duties and ethics, his ideas would lay the foundation for centuries of practicing civil servants. Like Socrates, he promoted a respect for culture and the pursuit of regular and good behavior. His students sought to realize moral obligations as they applied for official posts. Since rulers were looking for officials, who were ethical and could read and write, Confucianism evolved as the sole ideology of the Chinese state until the Marxist and Communist influences of the twentieth century.

Confucius thought man's behavior was the most important aspect in his philosophy, where virtue was of primary importance. He taught, *"where there is education, there are no classes,"* and education became important in Chinese culture. The ideal virtue required both a virtuous man and a virtuous society. Like the Greeks of the same period, he believed moral excellence led the Superior Man to become wise, benevolent and courageous.

In the fifth century BC, Mo Tzu emerged as a rival to Confucianism, and stressed the importance of universal altruism. Prior to the growth of Taoism, Moism and Confucianism dominated Chinese philosophy.

Like Plato who documented the ideas of Socrates, Chuang Tzu promoted the Taoist teachings of Lao Tzu. He presented imaginary dialogues, in which Lao Tzu opposed Confucius and the humanitarian moralists. Lao Tzu, a contemporary of Confucius, means Old Master, and he is credited with establishing the philosophical foundation of Taoism. Images of Lao Tzu show him riding a water buffalo. Perhaps this captured the idea of *Crossing the Great Water,* where perseverance in approaching the unknown strengthens one's awareness of *Tao.*

A more mystical version of Taoism evolved from the teachings of Chuang Tzu. Although the *Tao te Ching* had become a study of the *Way* to be used by rulers, Chuang Tzu revealed *Tao's* transformative power and developed a philosophy for the common people. The cycles of change that he observed at all levels of life that produced the different species he called *t'ien chun,* or "the Evolution of Nature." He romanced a transcendental awareness of *Tao* that went beyond perceptual boundaries, and taught that this was a prerequisite for becoming a sage. The following section reveals his influence on Taoism.

Chuang Tzu was often depicted as a rival to Hui Tzu, the great Logician. The conflict between his universality of spirit and Hui Tzu's grounded logic is dramatized in their many colorful discussions.

As they strolled one day, on the bridge over the river Hao, Chuang Tzu said, *"Look how the minnows dart here and there where they will. Such is the pleasure that fish enjoy."*

Hui Tzu replied logically, *"You are not a fish. How do you know what gives pleasure to fish?"*

Chuang Tzu countered with the same logical perspective, *"You are not I. How do you know that I do not know what gives pleasure to fish?"*

Hui Tzu stood firm, *"Just as I am not you, and cannot know whether you know, then because you are not a fish, you cannot know what gives pleasure to fish. My argument still holds."*

Chuang Tzu was undaunted. *"Then let us go back to where we started. You asked me how I knew what gives pleasure to fish. But you already knew how I knew it, when you asked me. You knew that I knew it, because we are standing here on the bridge at Hao."*

Chuang Tzu was a master at remaining at peace with life's fundamental harmony, while at the same time moving purposefully through the world. He must have been a great teacher because he is one of the most influential Taoist philosophers.

The conversations between the logician and the mystic present a clear example of how our systematic and rational mind is at odds with the part of us that might recognize our harmonious connection to what unfolds. The left-brain houses logic, creating classifications and distinctions, while the right brain processes impressions from a more holistic perspective.

After Hui Tzu's death, Chuang Tzu lamented, *"Since Hui Tzu died, I have had no proper stuff to work upon, have had no one with whom I can really talk."* The opposition arising from their colorful discourse demonstrates how individualistic growth is sharpened by the opportunity presented by contrasting ideas. Conflict always fires the furnaces of individuation and innovation.

Exploring the eight phenomena at the root of the *Book of Changes,* the masters recognized the *Creative* principle at the root of all manifestation. Since *Thunder* is arousing, it stirs the Creative out of dormancy. The *Wind* portrays the penetrating effort that cyclically transforms the wasteland for rebirth. *Fire,* like passion, has a synergistic connection to whatever keeps it burning. Inspired by a sense of peacefulness reflected in the *Joyous Lake,* they observed how *satisfaction* balances contentment with a devotion to movement. *Satisfaction* offsets a desire for the endless change that can arise from being unfulfilled, while *dissatisfaction* becomes the hunger pain that prods us toward change.

When we close to the evolutionary forces of life, the *Abysmal* captures the mystery of what remains locked within. The *Mountain* stands as the beginning and end because through stillness, we are made both, supple and strong. The Mountain can become the hardened perspective that keeps us a prisoner to the past, or the heights we climb to obtain a wider view. All signs of the Creative recede below the Earth at the onset of winter's incubation. Gestating in the womb of the *Yielding,* the Creative is reborn. The elements of *Tao* were associated with nature because nature revealed the purity of its ways.

The following section explores these eight evolutionary forces as they teach us to foster an innocent awareness that leads to a heightened perspective. As we approach the threshold of perception, we make the choice of what we will find. Only Earth or the Yielding is left out in these arrangements because Yielding is always a prerequisite for approaching the *gateway*. Whether we are letting go, or releasing past conditioning, in time, we must *turn back*. This backward movement allows us to approach the future with a *purity* of awareness. *"Knowing that which is to come requires backward movement."*

Receptivity ensures that our *te* is pliable enough to be cultivated. Exerting our will against the world can only disrupt harmony in following the *Way*. Just as life has a reason for meeting us halfway, at the threshold of perception, we bring nothing more than our *te* and a willingness to flow within the greater movement of life.

The Master said: "Silent fulfillment and confidence that needs no words depend upon virtuous conduct. The perfected nature will lead you to the gateway of life." At the gateway of life, we have the power to change our experiences.

SECTION FOUR

Approaching the Gateway: Principles 25-32

"Knowing that which is to come requires backward movement."

WU WANG Innocence

25th Degree: *If you do not know what cannot be done, you will accomplish great things.*

"Like a kite cut from the string,
lightly the soul of my youth has taken flight."
– Ishikawa Takuboku

"When you turn back, you are returned to a state of innocence." Approaching the gateway of perception, you can cherish the opportunity *not to know* so that you may *discover.* Baby birds do not develop their colorful beaks and feathers until adolescence, when it is time to leave the nest. Until then, their coloring allows them to remain hidden. Like a hatchling protected from early danger, when you approach the threshold of perception with a state of innocence, *"those who do not know what cannot be done can accomplish great things."*

Wu Wang means, "not attached," or "not caught up in defending yourself against unfolding events." Exerting the will can sometimes create turbulence in the river that leads you. When you are unattached, you can observe the fundamental harmony existing at all levels of life. The Master said: *"those who know no limits meet with no obstruction."*

Practicing *ming,* you can remove the barrier between *in here* and *out there.* It requires three things: compassion, appreciation and a willingness to follow. Having compassion when relating to others, you treat all experience as if it is a part of you. This is called owning your condition or taking personal responsibility for the events you face. Your appreciation for the *uncarved block,* or the ever-changing aspect of life that transcends definition makes you malleable in your observations and simple in your desires. If you do not play the host but remain the guest of a greater unfolding, you rule your empire without taking the lead, but instead, following. You can discover a new way of perceiving the world where backward movement, or a return to a state of innocence, will allow you to cultivate *that which is to come.*

The Master described ming: *"One who possesses virtue in abundance is comparable to a new born babe. The baby goes without knowing where it is going, and merges with the surroundings, moving along with it."* To observe things as they are, you will see how life is evolving, changing, and moving harmoniously in symbiotic ways. As you access this pure consciousness, Wu Wang is the image of not wasting time or avoiding by-paths that lead you astray. When you return to innocence, you are unattached to anything that would generate a response. *"Experience comes in while expression goes out."* When one faculty is engaged, the other is abandoned.

Transcending unnatural distinctions, the moment is now, you have arrived, and you are *just so*. You make the choice of whether you use the mind to establish boundaries or tear them down. Observing the emotions that stunt your ability to discover, trace their illusions and let them go. At this threshold, observe how anxiety and fear attach you to expectations about the future, while guilt and anger tie you to actions of the past. When you recognize and discard these responses, all that is left is innocence.

"Like a baby that has not learned to smile," move to that place before the response. Although *"desire brings you to observe life's manifestations,"* having no attachment to the passing scenery is the key to fostering an innocent awareness.

Evolution brings about variations, but these random changes rarely improve what is already working well. Creatures adapt in ways that are not always beneficial, and natural selection comes to *purge* mutations and reveals why the Way is described as turning back. As one of life's self-organizing systems, you seek stasis, while life leads you to transform. Every plant and animal on the earth has outlasted a struggle for existence that is three and a half billion years old. This means that moving forward without worry will not be second nature.

Wu wang, not attached, and wu wei, *"taking no unnatural action"* returns you to a state of peacefulness. Unattached to the past and not creating the response: *"I alone, am inactive and reveal no signs; listless as though I have no home to go back to."* The home you would have gone back to is the paradigm that would trap you in your growth.

TA CH'U Taming Power of the Great

26th Degree: *Your vital force is not wanting; only waiting for you to tap it.*

"We are told not to cross the bridge until we come to it,
but this world is owned by those who crossed bridges
in their imaginations far ahead of the crowd."

– Anonymous

"When innocence is present, it is possible to tame." Innocence cultivates virtue, yet virtue, when renewed daily, ensures a state of innocence. The Master said: *"The perfected nature, sustaining itself and enduring is the gateway of life."* An innocent perspective allows you to approach the gateway or threshold of perception to become *"the master of your experiences."* You tame your experiences by simply controlling your responses. *"The firm is able to keep strength still; this is great correctness."* Much time is spent preparing for and delivering your response. Only when you are not defending can you activate the Taming Power of the Great.

Responses are defensive tendencies that color how the world comes into view. You can change what the *"world will look and feel like,"* by approaching life without judgment. Every day you approach the gateway of perception, and choose what you will find.

The Master said: *"Do not listen with your ears, but listen with your mind. Do not listen with your mind, but listen with your vital force. Ordinary hearing does not go beyond the ears and the mind does not go beyond its symbols. Your vital force is not wanting but waiting. Life brings together all that is void to itself. Be empty, that is all. Thus you can master things and not be injured by them."*

When you tame your desires, *"not eating at home brings good fortune,"* because you move beyond your perceptual routines to be nourished by discovery. Gather the energy of desire's outward attachment and tap it as the *inner fuel* that activates the powerful peacefulness that comes forward by simply *being.* Stand at the threshold, connect with your vital force and observe. Find comfort in a strength that needs no words.

In China, the lion protected the forests, and its statue was used to protect the gates and temples. Another gatekeeper, the Dragon Carp, had only one goal: *crossing the Dragon Gate.* Beyond this Gate, many believed paradise could be found. Like the salmon, the carp swims upstream and jumps the rapids, and symbolized human advancement and achievement in life. The Dragon Carp is a constant reminder of the pursuit of excellence, reflecting how following instinct makes you powerful. Whereas the lion symbolized great passion and fearlessness, the carp was a symbol of *instinctual perseverance.* Te, when fortified, becomes a power that is sufficient under any circumstance.

Transcending the illusion of how you must conquer and take, you can develop the powerful peacefulness that comes when you no longer see the world as a place full of obstacles, but as your home.

The tree requires turbulent storms for regeneration, and every seed must release its outer covering when forced to push against rocks and stones. You too, are being led like the creatures that feel the cold as a call for hibernation, and how spring brings them back from migration. Just as the plant instinctively knows the time to flower, you are fundamentally connected to the place in which you thrive. As life coaxes your real nature forward, adversity, like the changing climate that shapes your character, merely carves away the layers that keep it hidden.

Te is your instinctual endowment and connection to life. When cultivated alongside of fearlessness, it is like water that finds its own course without any sense of barriers. Water can dissolve mountains and evens out, regardless of where it flows. The power of te connects you to the germinating power of life. Transcending the gate or the illusion of obstacles leads to a type of paradise in consciousness. This paradise is simply a place without boundaries.

As the Creative rises within, *"it furthers one to cross the great water."* A change in perspective allows you to see obstacles as the banks of a great river that is always moving you forward. Even when you fail, you are left with something that becomes necessary for your growth. The Creative within the Mountain suggests the strong creative power that is hidden like a treasure. The Taming Power of the Great rises when you become content in your power. When you re-evaluate the obstacle, *"dimly visible, it only seemed as if it were there."*

Life's secret is that it has been committed to your success since the beginning. To take no action that is unnatural to your instinctive nature ensures that you will meet with no resistance.

"Generating movement even in the hardest things is how the great is tamed. Creating movement even in the greatest things is what makes Tao mysteriously powerful. The most submissive thing in the world can ride roughshod over the hardest in the world – that which is without substance enters that which has no crevices."

I Nourishing

27th Degree: *Ignorance is the night of the mind, but a night without moon and star.*

> *"Everyone sees the unseen in proportion to the clarity of the heart, and that depends upon how much one has polished it. Whoever has polished it more, sees more – more unseen forms become manifest."*
>
> *– Rumi*

"The Arousing Thunder moves within the Mountain." It suggests how thought is excited into action. The Master said: *"What the people determine as great, they nourish."* From a perspective of innocence and by taming your responses, you can begin to shape the world you are growing into. All you nourish in thought becomes your experiences; change your thoughts and experience will be different.

The energy of thought becomes manifestation simply in how you interpret events. Many people can witness the same event, but each will project a different experience. *"To know what is important to the person, one must only observe what they actively cultivate."* Although you come to give life labels, *"the Way passes through the mouth without flavor."*

If you are open to growth, you will see the Way as being good; if you are not, you will call it bad. Yet, it remains without distinction.

You can observe the person by what they nourish. *"A person who understands the Way will conform to the Way. A person who lives by the rules of others will conform to the rules of others. A person who knows only loss will conform to loss."* Nourishing presents the image of a mouth, where ideas go in and words comes out. What you nourish in your heart and mind becomes the image of ingesting and sustaining your experiences. If you want to experience life differently, begin to approach life differently.

Polish the mysterious mirror that reflects the condition of your inner world onto events. When it is without blemish, you will discover the meaning behind what unfolds.

A student watched a bee, spinning upside down in a shallow pond. When it began to drown, he pulled it out, and was stung. The Master watched as another bee crawled into the pond. When it started to drown, the student pulled it out and was stung again.

The Master asked, *"Why do you keep doing the same thing, when each time the bee stings you in return?"*

The student replied, *"It is the bee's nature to sting, but it is my nature to save it."*

What you repeatedly do comes to define your character. If you are not happy with events, observe the things you do to create them.

Both nuclear trigrams emerge as the Receptive Earth suggesting how habitual thoughts are mirrored to become experience.

You receive nourishment or reward in many ways, but this sustenance merely reflects how you sustain your way of living. If the outcome or response to your actions is always the same, then you must derive *some benefit from it,* or you would change your actions.

You have the power to shape your experiences simply in the way you approach them. Your destiny unfolds from a seed within, although life will always meet you half way, with the events that will help you discover it. When you are sincere in your te and remaining open in your response, nothing ever comes to block your way.

"The Way is easy, yet people prefer by-paths." You can know what your path will look like by what you nourish.

As the Creative is aroused within, you have the opportunity to observe what motivates you, and what you nourish at the root of each experience. At the threshold of perception, *"pay heed to what you provide with nourishment, and to what you seek."* Chances are you will find it.

TA KUO Overwhelming of the Great

28th Degree: *To follow the energy of life, you will discover that it is always seeking the best of what you can be.*

"The study of Nature is intercourse with the Highest Mind.

You should never trifle with Nature."

–Louis Agassiz

"Nourishing something without putting it to proper use, will finally evoke movement in the image of the great becoming overwhelming." Like a heavy roof that rests upon a weak foundation, the structure sags in the middle and will collapse. Unbalanced energy always generates a chain reaction. A series of events ensue, in which each event is both the result of the one preceding, and the cause of what follows. Ta Kuo demonstrates that protecting a weak or inauthentic foundation is no match for the power of nature to bring it down.

Nature, in its Creative form, explores diversity by bringing opposites together. At the same time, a constant movement of the Yielding takes form in life's pursuit of balance. When you defend yourself against Creative change, you are forced to become Yielding. Floating along Yielding to your beliefs, events will force you to embrace Creative change. When either is overly demonstrated, the other emerges to strike a balance. As you project your sense of right and wrong on each experience, you operate from a weak foundation. In the chain reaction of events, observe how life is always taking its natural course.

There is a profound harmony in the earth's inter-dependent

systems. Animals take in energy as food and oxygen, and discard it as heat, carbon dioxide and waste. Bacteria and fungus process the waste back into plants. These plants take in carbon dioxide and use it to build their own substances through photosynthesis, which releases oxygen within the carbon dioxide. Animals breathe in the oxygen and exhale carbon dioxide that returns to nourish the plants.

At the same time that you observe harmony in these self-organizing systems, we witness mating collisions, battles for sustenance, and eruptions reflecting the earth's fundamental transformative power. From the standpoint of regeneration, these processes *"diverge in nature as they issue forth, but are the same."*

Progress will always demand that some things fail, while others succeed. Yet, those who fail are also made stronger. Your image of a perfect world might reduce it to one of degeneration. Rather than defend the idea of right or wrong, simply remain a student of nature. *"When 'this' and 'that' have no opposites,"* you discover order in the turning.

After being hunted to near extinction in Yellowstone National Park, wolves were reintroduced to control the exploding bison and elk populations, and a chain reaction ensued. Biologists recorded numerous scavengers, including animals, birds and insects feeding on the new carcasses. They discovered an impact on the food chain not previously appreciated.

Once the park reverted to a more natural environment, the elk were again prey. They moved more, and grazed less on the willows, which also began to thrive. The flourishing willows allowed beavers to build dams that transformed small meadows into lakes. Fish, waterfowl and other insects began to thrive. Protecting the elk and bison from being the top of the food chain is like *"nourishing something without putting it to proper use."* This unnatural intervention caused a chain reaction that denied sustenance to a myriad of creatures. On an even more profound level, we were interfering with life's natural drive to explore the best of what it might become.

When the excessive overwhelms the weak, the weak will rise in a chain reaction, whether in the realm of politics, the natural world, or within the paradigm of the individual.

The combination of Creative power and the moving Wind, are lost within the Lake in the idea of joyous oblivion. From within you, the Creative seeks expression and being naturally yourself is your only option.

The Master said: *"if you must stand alone, be unconcerned. If you must renounce the world, be undaunted."* Authenticity can only manifest when you move beyond the idea of right and wrong. By following the wisdom of nature, you return to the pathway and *"use no counting rods."* Overcoming judgment returns you to the natural way.

K'AN The Abysmal

29th Degree: *If you cannot change the direction of the wind, adjust your sails and let it take you.*

"For the benefit of the flowers, we water the thorns too."

– Egyptian Proverb

"Things cannot stay in a state of critical mass. If movement does not occur, what follows is the Abysmal." The Abysmal Water is above and below, revealing a flooding ravine that suggests peril. *"The water flows uninterrupted toward its goal."* While life coaxes you toward gentle transformation, you can refuse, although events will take you there anyway. K'an shows that a lack of movement orchestrates a chain of events that will sweep you back into the great river.

Without trusting in the flow of events, the situation becomes threatening, but only in proportion to the disparity that exists between *the necessary transition* and your *fear of going there.* It is in the things you cannot change, that you discover life's power to guide you.

Faced with the devastation of the old way, you are pulled back into life's great river. When the storms set in, you will realize how much energy was wasted in worrying about each, and every squall. The Master said: *"What is tightly held in the arms cannot slip loose,"* although when the waters are raging, you will let go. Sometimes it is only through the Abysmal that your arms are opened, and your hands set free. Whatever remains, will return you to sincerity, while deepening your connection to life.

Some see the destructive pattern of our relationship to the earth like a disease. Resembling pathogens, we have created a rash by under-mining its mountains and tearing out its trees. We have given the earth a fever as temperatures rise in proportion to the emissions that we put into the atmosphere. The earth seeks to cleanse itself with weather patterns that become more severe. As our waste products contaminate its normal metabolic processes, we challenge its ability to maintain resistance. We actually fund its enormous power to cleanse itself through floods, hurricanes and torrential rains. Yet, pollution is destructive to our well-being too, and life is always teaching us about ourselves.

In the image of a dangerous gorge that draws water downward, K'an also portrays wings and a hat. Your thoughts are given wings that can either trap or release you. Identifying the barriers that you construct to ward off change, recognize how nature's power to dissolve them will come in equal measure.

The freedom to keep moving becomes important in achieving wellness. K'an can reduce all of life to its most fundamental and simple aspects. When the Abysmal rushes in, the Way is made clear again. You can cling to the floating debris of an outworn way of thinking, but will find that it is useless in your new way of approaching the world.

Although it rises in rain, water has a tendency to flow earthward, and is the image of remaining grounded and natural. All that remains after the Abysmal will be your deeply profound connection to life.

LI The Clinging Fire

30th Degree: *When you can appreciate nature's power to break through all barriers, you will discover that this same power is inside of you.*

"Life is a pure flame, and we live by an invisible sun within us."
– Thomas Browne

"The clinging means resting on something." As the Abysmal Water flows into the pit, you search for something to cling to. Li is the image of a Clinging Fire that seeks something to keep it burning. The Fire above and below reveals how everything in the universe moves synergistically with everything else. You believe that you can find a frame of reference in some point of the past yet it too, ever gives way. You must therefore, find something more meaningful to rest upon.

What emerges from any difficult transition is the discovery of *that thing,* which will guide and support you when all else is taken away. Although events *out there* orchestrate the changes, they merely lead you to cultivate a shift of awareness *in here.* The Master said: *"The cultivation of the self consists in the rectification of the mind."* After the Abysmal, you can reconnect with the fire within, This is the essence of te, and it holds you to the center of your unique pattern of development.

After the Abysmal, you often arrive at the *suchness* existing at every moment, without the need to look any further. You realize, "what is…is," and stop fighting the very thing that reveals your power. *"Life is like a flowing river; identify its current to know contentment."*

Nature moves freely and spontaneously toward change and the pursuit of harmony. Obstruction only appears when you classify life in terms of good, bad, right or wrong, but the idea of obstruction is a man made illusion. Life is blind to the idea of obstacles, except in the way that it overcomes them.

The unnatural things you build to obstruct life's forward progress will never be a match for its enormous power to break them down. Even water will immediately break down the molecules of whatever substance it encounters. All things have a purpose, whether or not you can appreciate it at the time. Li is the expression in attitude and behavior of the great power that makes the world what it is. Whether nature is removing the outworn, or building something new, it is always productive.

The force driving nature toward renewal is inside of you. It funds your te, and when you can cultivate it, you will discover a world that supports your success. In Li, ming evolves into *ching,* or the powerful peacefulness that is ever-present, skillful and capable of generating success that knows no boundaries. Whereas ming keeps your perception pure, ching activates the germinating power of te. Rather than emulate nature's ways, you can access its tremendous power as your vital force, and make *"contact with it like a bubbling spring."*

Fire is dependent upon whatever it uses to keep burning. Observe how you remain dependant upon circumstances to strengthen what you already know, and then let it all go.

You will discover that limitations always enable yo
your brightness. To know success, you must only stoke the Fire of you
vital force. The Master said: *"When the mind is like a mirror, it grasps nothing, refuses nothing, receives, but does not keep."* To approach the gateway, you can use the mind as a portal or a prison. When you *"unblock the openings,"* you can view a world bathed beneath the power of your inner light.

HSIEN Influence

31st Degree: *Wooing is how you attract those things that you desire.*

"Great hearts steadily send forth the secret forces
that incessantly draw great events."
– Emerson

"The Lake on the Mountain: the image of influence where the weak is above and the strong is below." Like gravity or weak nuclear forces, we observe how something that appears inconsequential still activates the enormous power of attraction. As you become aware of how you woo experience, your power grows productively. Since you always attract the things you need, you can meet circumstances Joyful like the Lake where energy is not exhausted in defensive arguments and depleting conquests.

Hsien is the image of knowing your advantageous position because of a firm and steadfast foundation. We see the Mountain bowing down to the Joyous Lake as the idea of courtship and the lesson of the strong wooing the weak. The Joyous Lake offers its gentle rivers and streams to bring life to the Mountain. In return, the Mountain allows the water to be preserved as snow until it is needed downstream.

Influence presents the idea of balance and power. If you are content in your power, it will be fortified without having te exert any energy. From the delicate spider's web to the dandelion seeds that ride upon the wind for regeneration, nature achieves success through a type of wooing.

In the image of two broken pieces of pottery that fit together perfectly, a partnership with life is formed at the threshold of perception. *"When you leave the mind alone and allow it to function in its most spontaneous and natural way, te will develop authentically."* Just as there is a driving force behind life's pursuit of excellence, te is your transformative essence and evolving power *to become*. When you observe and accept things as they really are, you are no longer defending anything. This will allow your real nature to come forward without obstruction.

Moving away from the negativity of "what you shouldn't do," you can attract by virtue of "what you do." In this spontaneous and unfettered perspective, your entire being is given expression. You will discover how the pathway always mirrors your capabilities.

Lieh Tzu was trained by Lao Shang: *"For three years, my mind did not reflect upon right or wrong and my lips did not speak of gain or loss. During this time, my Master bestowed only one glance upon me. After five years, a change took place, and my mind did reflect on right and wrong; my lips spoke of gain and loss. For the first time, my Master relaxed his countenance and smiled. After seven years, I let my mind reflect on whatever it would, but it no longer occupied itself with right or wrong. I let my lips utter whatsoever they pleased, but they no longer spoke of gain or loss. Then, at last, my Master invited me to sit on the mat beside him. After nine years, my mind gave free reign to its reflections; my mouth gave free reign to its speech. Of right, wrong, gain or loss, I had no knowledge. Internal and external were blended in unity. I was wholly unaware of what my body was resting upon. I was born this way, like leaves falling from a tree and playing on the wind. In fact, I knew not whether the wind was riding on me, or whether I was riding on the wind."*

Nature explores variations that are not immediately beneficial, and in the process, perfects itself. Oxygen appeared two billion years ago, and was fatal to the life forms at that time. Bacteria are an example of a life form that did not develop the defensive protein necessary to render its effects harmless. Yet today, oxygen is necessary for the survival of most species.

When you open to the *Nature's Way of Success*, spontaneity or a willingness to make mistakes will enhance your growth. If you do not hold back, you will be in a better position to receive. By not classifying experience in terms of good and bad, you are freed from thought that can become restrictive.

"Like attracts like; obstruction attracts obstruction." By wooing, you activate a spontaneous attraction that is always reciprocated. Whether it is the lover, who opens to love, or the farmer, who uses the seasons to plant, all that you reap is directly tied to your intention.

HENG Duration

32nd Degree: *Commitment is the force of attraction that brings all things back to you.*

"Tis not the many oaths that make the truth;
but the plain single vow, that is vowed true."
– Shakespeare

"Relationships should be long lasting; therefore follows the principle of duration." The Thunder and Wind mutually Arouse movement in a synergistic portrayal of something that is enduring and constant. The principles of Innocence to Wooing allow us to observe the way in which what we experience is determined by how we approach the threshold of perception.

In the image of Thunder and Wind, the climate is changing. Whatever is unnecessary will be uprooted, while life strengthens what will endure. In the nuclear trigrams, the Joyous Lake and the Creative portray firmness in joy. Regardless of the changes, a perspective firm in joy will experience joy.

Commitment gives durability to the changes and a commitment to openness requires daily discipline.

Nature is composed of the hidden movement of the unseen. We *see* the Lightning but fail to *see* the Thunder of expanding air. We watch branches move by an invisible Wind. We cannot see the *force* but observe its *effects.* In the same way, commitment is not tangible, but its effects are recognizable. We either get it done or come up with excuses for why we failed. A commitment to openness gives durability to *that which is to come.*

In Heng, commitment gives duration to the spontaneous attraction existing between a heart centered in te and the experience, which makes it stronger.

"When you act from benevolence, it will feel good; it will feel like self-realization." Benevolence allows you to open harmoniously to life with the knowledge that you are deeply connected to what unfolds. This is obvious when you make a commitment to your spouse. Fulfilling their needs is inseparable from fulfilling your own. Only when both of you are fulfilled, do you experience *personal* contentment in the relationship.

Benevolence is an unconditional appreciation for *what is,* and keeps you rooted to the moment. Union brings two things together to make them one. In this case, your inner perspective is joined with experience. Whether in relationships or when meeting events, *"stand firm and do not change direction."* Commitment is the force of attraction that brings all things back to you. *"Fix the mind on an end that endures"* and your joy will be unwavering.

You are carried through life as the image of a boat and a heart between two shores. The two shores are how you travel between good and bad, right and wrong, emptiness and fullness as you classify your journey. In reality, they are merely the banks of one great river. Life is powerful and good; it is profoundly committed to your success, but you must remain committed to meeting events half way. The heart suggests sincerity and what connects you to the germinating power of life.

A duality of perspective can make you separate what is fundamentally united. Commitment, like the joining of man and wife, is a change in awareness that makes benevolence or *firmness in joy* a pathway to self-realization.

Like the highs and lows and the vicissitudes of emotions spent during courtship, once a commitment is established, the Way becomes much easier. *"Knowing that which is to come"* is made easier by the simple act of devotion.

SECTION FIVE

Movement in Stillness: Principles 33-40

"Without doing anything, nothing is undone."

TUN Retreat

33rd Degree: *Content in your power, you have no need to engage the obstacle.*

"A quarrel is quickly settled when deserted by one party:

there is no battle unless there be two."

– Seneca

"Things do not remain forever in their place. Therefore follows retreat." Retreat means withdrawing. When difficulty arises, retreating allows you to conserve energy and accentuate your power. Similar to martial arts where you tap the momentum of the opponent, movement in stillness allows you to gain without expending energy. *"Content in your power, you have no need to engage the obstacle."*

"Mountain under the Creative: the image of retreat. The wise keep the inferior at a distance, not angrily, but with reserve." When you are firm in your power, you often become a vehicle for another's growth. Life has a reason for bringing firm energy together. Since two things that are firm do not deviate much, chances are good they will eventually meet in

the river of life. Yet, if you are content in your power, you will have no need to engage firmness or contention in another.

"Retreat means success. In what is small, perseverance furthers." A grand demonstration of power is not necessary. Retreat requires care and an appreciation of your integrity and te. Tun is an image of a pig, representing contentment and well-being, combined with the idea of walking away. You are not rude and indifferent; if you do not become defensive, the other party cannot pull you into a confrontation. They meet with no resistance and therefore, do not contend. This captures how *"when you open, all obstacles disappear."* By not doing anything, nothing needs to be undone.

In martial arts, one learns economy of movement and how to move in a centered position where balance is never threatened. By holding to a specific position, the opponent is kept at a disadvantage, enabling one to maximize strength. In this case, you hold to your character or integrity. As a principle of movement in stillness, Tun is the image of purposeful withdrawal. Retreat does not mean giving up, but allows you to strengthen your ability to remain open, while firm in your character.

When you come up against any barrier, engaging the obstacle always gives it power. *"The wise meet all opposition with a quiet mind and open heart. Then all opposition naturally disappears. Without doing anything, nothing is undone."* Action can trigger endless reaction that may need to be undone. This is the great power of *not doing*. Purposeful withdrawal will disconnect you from a charged situation that might deplete you of the integrity of your te. *"Perseverance in small matters brings success."* Small matters take place within, and integrity fortifies character so that your nature remains incorruptible.

Observing nature, you may sometimes feel some things are not as they should be. Yet, eventually you recognize how nature also turns back to regenerate, rather than always displaying obvious forward growth. Even while you are open to growth, turning back is also a pathway forward. *"The sheerest whiteness seems sullied. The great vessel takes long to complete."* The great vessel holds your te as you travel through the river of life.

TA CHUANG The Power of the Great

34th Degree: *If you are steadfast in your power, you cannot be thrown from your center.*

"A suppressed resolve will betray itself in the eyes."

– George Elliot

"Things cannot retreat forever. Hence follows the idea of the power of the great." When you are firm in openness and character, you will expand inwardly to develop a power that will lead to greater outward movement. The Creative is strong as it pushes upward, toward the Arousing Thunder. This union of movement and power reveals how *stillness* activates the power of the great. *"When you lose the self, you need only return to stillness."*

"The meaning of the power of the great shows itself in the fact that one pauses." Ta Chuang is another aspect of movement in stillness, where one steadfast in te is never thrown from their center when confronted by events. One reveals the *"constant virtue that is always sufficient."* It ensures that you act benevolently because defensiveness is reflection of weakness. The Master said: *"Mysterious virtue is far reaching, but when things turn back, it turns back with them."* That which cannot be accomplished through force will be fortified through stillness.

Many myths describe a hero, abandoned or separated from royal parents, and forced to grow up as an ordinary child. You too, can feel abandoned and thrown into a world that does not understand you. Heeding a call from within, you embark on a great journey and ultimately discover your real identity. Although you travel across dangerous terrains in the journey of a lifetime, once you arrive, you realize this discovery could have taken place in our backyard. Yet, the actual journey *out there* had the effect of changing you *in here.* It opens you to the understanding that "your way" was only one way.

"If you are a valley to the empire, then the constant virtue will be sufficient." To be a valley to the empire is to be composed and willing to bow down in every situation. Your constant virtue does not require that you defend it: *it is just so.* When strength surpasses the turning point, there is a danger that one may rely on power heedless of what is right, yet *"without rightness, there can be no greatness."* You are always activating the power of attraction. Sincerity keeps your experiences real

so that you have no need to defend anything. One willing to bow down or concede in the face of opposition is demonstrating ultimate power.

Vigilant in your te, you will find yourself on a pathway where nothing needs to be undone. *"Lay hold of this truth and you can be master of your present existence."*

The germinal seed blossoms from a foundation of sincerity and benevolence. *"The penetration of germinal thought into the mind promotes the workings of the mind. When this working furthers and brings peace to life, it elevates one's nature. Whatever goes beyond this indeed transcends all knowledge. When one comprehends nature and understands the transformations, one lifts the character to the level of the miraculous."*

The sage on the pathway of greatness has no need to demonstrate force. Great success comes when your benevolent nature allows you to transform the obstacle into an opportunity to fortify your integrity. This productive power magnetizes the opportunity to use it. Thus, you become great.

Movement in stillness becomes the image of bowing down with the knowledge of a power that cannot be threatened. The Power of the Great does not need to be demonstrated or proven; it is always sufficient. Just as you gather and tame your passions for productive use, you compose your te in the same way. You again achieve great movement without doing anything out of the ordinary. Success happens naturally because of your constant virtue or character.

CHIN Progress

35th Degree: *A foundation without prejudice is the first step in how the weak progresses.*

"Every separate thought takes shape and
becomes visible in color and form."
– Liu Hua-Yang

"Beings do not stay in a state of power. Hence follows progress, which means expansion." To progress without the outward demonstration of force is how you expand outwardly, by activating *the power that is sufficient.*

We tend to measure strength in the same way that we measure force. Force moves bodies and is actively creating a reaction. If we push on something and cause it to move, the force we exert also propels us backward. Strength utilizes a power that may appear weak and yet, its power comes from yielding. Force can exhaust energy, but strength grows exponentially. Being yielding, all energy that is no longer wasted by defending yourself against events *out there* becomes productive *in here.* The more productive your energy is *in here,* the more powerful you become *out there.*

Movement in stillness fortifies te because it is not exhausted. Strength is not measured by overcoming others, but by overcoming yourself. *"Those who master others have force; those who master themselves have strength."* By cultivating inner strength, the weak progresses to unprecedented heights, in the image of outward expansion.

The Master described one of extreme power: *"When a drunken man falls from his carriage, no matter how fast it is traveling, he is never killed. His bones and joints are no different from other men, but because he did not know that he was riding, he does not know that he has fallen out."* Unruffled by the changing scenery, power is not a measure of the force you exert; rather, it is the measure of your connection to the profound germinating power within. *"Only when you stop trying, will you discover that you are simply doing. Be natural, that is all."*

Once a pupil of Lao Tzu settled in Wei-lei and hired servants that showed no intelligence and handmaidens who were selfish. The botchy and bloated shared his house; the dithering and fumbling waited upon him. After three years, the crops in Wei-lei began to flourish. The people said, "When he came, we thought him stupidly eccentric but now the day is not long enough to count our blessings." In time, the people wanted to treat him as ruler, but he refused and said: "When the breath of spring comes, the hundred plants begin to grow and during autumn, we harvest its treasure. So long as the Way works unimpeded, spring and autumn cannot fail at their task." He was unaware of the discriminations the townspeople placed on each other. *"Spring never fails in its task;"* was all that he knew. Without the need to pass judgment on the things around you, your steadfast virtue and trust in the Way unleashes success at the same time others are crippled by negativity and failure.

Chin is the image of birds taking flight as the sun begins to rise. It happens naturally, day after day, without great ceremony; *it is what they do.* Spiders portray the proper relationship to life. They build a b and simply wait for life to bring them nourishment. They ɜnd with anything, and are unconcerned with what has not landed in the web. Tiny seeds too, portray the progressive power of the weak accomplished through movement in stillness. Their nature leads them to grow intricate spikes that will attach to the fur of passing animals. To follow life, you must build your foundation by cultivating whatever unique qualities life has given to you. You can then embrace the wondrous things life brings to nourish you.

MING I Darkening of the Light

36th Degree: *When the world grows dark, your inner light is given definition.*

"I prefer winter and fall, when you feel the bone structure of the landscape,
the loneliness of it – the dead feeling of winter.
Something waits beneath it – the whole story doesn't show."

– Andrew Wyeth

"Expansion will certainly meet with resistance. Therefore follows the darkening of the light." As the Clinging Fire sinks below the Receptive Earth, Ming I portrays how we must sometimes operate in darkness to find our inner light. Like the time of winter, the situation requires that you turn back to stoke the fire within. Even while your power is growing, you still experience the friction of life's natural tension that keeps you evolving. If this power is real, it will endure. You can face adversity as if life is asking you a question about the sincerity of your actions. Your answer may be, " . .Yes…it is good…it is real, and nothing

can threaten it." If this is true, it will endure. In this, *"the way that is bright seems dark."*

Regardless of the circumstances, something within is cultivated so that you may shine brightly. Keeping the inner light of te burning, Ming I is an image of the sun and moon, and a threat by an archer, who is no match for these great luminaries. The sun is your inner light and clarity, while the moon represents how it reflects it upon experience. Although the light may appear dim outwardly, it grows within and nothing can threaten it.

That which is cultivated through difficulty grows like a seed beneath the soil of your inner light. *"We tend to hide what we dislike about ourselves and display the beautiful. In this way, what is good is put on parade and wasted, while we nurture and hold tightly to what is ugly."* Outwardly searching for acceptance and appreciation will lead you to become a mere reflection of what you believe the world expects of you. Instead of the flowering of your beautiful nature, a weed will take root within and grow. When you are not authentic, you discover why *"those who go against the way end up being called unlucky."*

"One that is born beautiful and not given a mirror or told of their beauty will not know that they are more beautiful than others. Beauty will simply be a part of their nature. What happens of its own accord is like the leader who simply loves the people. Without fame or being told of their graces, love is their nature. The sage does not hide away in the woods and hills. What is hidden is our te. One can interact with the world without losing the self."

When the environment grows dark, the moon captures the sun's reflection. This is an example of a greater power that can remain hidden. Sometimes the light within can only be revealed in contrast to the darkening of the light outside. *"Do not be sad. Turning back is how the Way moves."* Movement in stillness is how you stoke the fire within regardless of the changes in your environment. Veiling the light becomes an image of protecting the character and keeping it sacred.

CHIA JEN The Family

37th Degree: *In the contrast of your family, life reveals your deepest color.*

"To put the family in order, we must cultivate our personal life;
and to cultivate our personal life, we must first set our hearts right."

– Confucius

"During times of adversity, we turn back to the family." The Gentle Wind stirs above the Clinging Fire, fanning it and sustaining its illumination. Chia Jen is the hearth fire, kept burning during times of trouble. It is a place where you find safety and nourishment during difficult times. The Clinging Fire shows your dependence on the family, and within this small circle, you may observe your reactive character in the larger aspect of society. You may think you are only different in family dynamics, but this is not true. Heat creates energy. The Wind stirs it up and excites it. The truthfulness of the family circle simply has a way of activating your dynamics *more quickly*.

All things your family holds sacred endure for you throughout your life. Chia Jen is the image of a pig and a dog, protected under a dwelling, while someone prays. The pig represents all that you hold dear, while the dog is your faithfulness. Even as the Wind of experience continues to shape your character, the root of your inner clarity and te emerged when you were young. Chia Jen suggests the dwelling, which protects all that you hold sacred.

Natural selection drives divergence in character traits because the more diversified we are, the better is our chance of survival. Even among family members within a particular species, each are endowed with unique variations. This ensures competition for short supply in a shared environment is always minimized.

The Master said: *"All things are complete in oneself. There is no greater joy than to examine oneself and be sincere. Sincere in thought and action, what reason is there for self-pity?"* You may seek encouragement from your family and not find it. You believe they will provide a haven and instead, they give you a stone. This stone becomes your gift, because it will shape you into the individual nature designed you to be. The family can be a source of support, even while their dynamics shape you in the same way that water polishes a stone. In the contrast of your differences, they often reveal your deepest color. You stand in the present as life's best example of *one* variation of the line you carry forward. Just as the Wind and the Flame glow brightest near the hearth, reflected in the differences among your family, you discover just how *unique* you are.

K'UEI Opposition

38th Degree: *Life's natural friction is the force that shapes your individuality.*

"He that wrestles with us strengthens our nerve,
and sharpens our skill. Our antagonist is our helper."
– Edmund Burke

"In family gatherings, we find that misunderstandings arise from habitual behavior, thus we see the principle of opposition." Habitual behavior can lead to stagnation, while nature appears to work against this tendency. Your conditioning can best be observed in family dynamics, which allows you to see a snapshot of the defensive tendencies you carry forward in life. Regardless of the opposition, life is always further defining variations through opposition.

K'uei is the movement in stillness that allows you to observe what happens when opposites meet. It is not the pleasant exchanges you remember, but the unpleasant ones that can stay with you for days, months and years. While you may cherish times of harmony, through difficulty real growth occurs. Even when someone seems to be challenging you, they are also helping you to further define your individuality. Eventually you will discover a power and way of being that is *just so.*

When you move beyond the idea that life is a place of polarities, you will begin to see opposition as life's movement toward a higher unity. The Clinging Flame burns above the Joyous Lake as an image of clarity reflected upon the vicissitudes of experience. Life explores variety and change through contrast. At the same time, it releases accumulating energy by stagnant energy together.

In the natural world, opposition is the universal face of changing phenomena. When you open to its creative and regenerative pull, you discover life's pursuit of novelty, not its polarities. At all levels of life, friction always releases and disburses bound up energy. The Master said: *"opposition is a prerequisite for union."* Two people who prefer to sweep issues under the carpet will never discover authentic union. Confucius taught that opposites are merely two different aspects of a higher unity.

When we clash, we identify our differences that give form to our unique qualities. As we bridge our differences, we marry our separate wills toward a common purpose. Through this blending of wills, a higher unity takes form. Yet, this transformation could not materialize without the diverging energy that appears in the form of opposition. This friction is life's evolutionary tension that keeps all things evolving.

In each species, if the masculine and feminine meet, there is usually reproduction. Opposite elements that retain their unique nature in coming together, eventually sharpen and define each other's individuality. When life moves toward contrast, whatever is dormant is excited to the surface so that it can be applied for productive use.

bstruction

39th Degree: *Adversity is how life unleashes your excellence from within.*

"You cannot teach a man anything;

you can only help him to find it within."

– Galileo

"Through opposition, difficulties arise in the form of obstruction." Behind you is the Mountain of Keeping Still, while ahead of you is the Abysmal Water. Without delving below its mysterious surface, you cannot proceed because there is something unknown to be discovered. Even while opposition leads to harmony and innovation, union eventually gives way to renewal. Life brings elements together to explore a higher unity, but in time, it also comes to separate stagnation.

Whether in your personal or professional life, obstructions that block your forward progress are simply nature's pursuit of a better way. You can curse circumstances and apply your will in a futile attempt to ward off change. On the other hand, you can allow the obstruction to reveal how you might achieve movement in a more innovative way. If you want to get across the Water, you must explore a new way of doing so. Like anything else in the natural world, the path of your evolution will only be limited by your unwillingness to change.

"Acting from knowledge of the constant, keeps one impartial;" you do not meet with difficulty because you do not see it as such. You can observe a world that is *becoming,* where everything must become stronger. Adversity is simply how life unleashes your excellence from

within: something *out there* makes you grow *in here.* Obstruction out there is always an opportunity for something new.

When you encounter difficulty, remain still enough to discover how the obstacle is an opportunity to expand. *"Obstruction means difficulty. The danger is ahead. To see the danger and know how to stand still, that is wisdom."* Keeping Still is the only way to recognize how the situation is transforming.

Chien portrays someone limping with cold feet because circulation has been impeded. Cold feet symbolize fear and a lack of movement, and impeding circulation indicates that something is causing a blockage to the natural flow. You can flail about in the waters of change or remain still to allow the water to lead you.

The Master said: *"The path that leads one to encounter further obstruction becomes the only danger."* Obstruction is always an indication that change is necessary. You may be limping along a path of extreme resistance, when a different route might be more appropriate and *easier.* If you discover the path of least resistance, you will find your way.

Like the Chinese image of crisis, which combines danger with opportunity, there is always the danger of continuing, or the opportunity to change direction. You may perceive obstruction as a barrier to your progress, but if you climb upon it to achieve a broader view, you will see that it is an opportunity and not a barrier.

In Chien, inner movement is shaped by stillness so that the obstruction actually leads you away from the path of danger. It is only dangerous because it is unnatural to believe that anything can withstand the forces of change. In this situation, you will discover why *"those who go against the Way meet with constant difficulty."*

HSIEH Deliverance

40th Degree: *There is no real difficulty that requires outward movement.*

"Within yourself deliverance must be searched for,
because each man makes his own prison."
–Sir Edwin Arnold

"Things cannot remain permanently obstructed, therefore follows deliverance and the release of tension." The Arousing Thunder stirs over the Abysmal Water in the image of a sudden storm, which relieves atmospheric pressure.

Hsieh is the image of a sharp instrument, which loosens knots. You can be *"worn and newly made,"* when you release the unproductive energy that remains connected to anger. Anger is always weighted against the measure of tomorrow; if you cannot let something go, you are forced to carry it with you. How much productive and joyful energy is wasted in the process?

As the last principle of movement in stillness, you find deliverance is the liberation that comes from releasing your hold on the past. In the case of forgiveness, you give nothing away, that you really need anyway.

When you hold onto anger, it becomes your burden and dissipates as unproductive energy. Through forgiveness, you can move freely, unhampered by unnecessary baggage. This is how anger becomes a shackle as you attempt to walk a pathway of freedom.

As clouds gather, electricity generates moisture, and the atmosphere is filled with an unproductive heaviness. The ensuing storm releases the tension and cleanses the earth, so all things can breath freely again. All of the principles of movement in stillness teach you how there is no real difficulty that requires action *out there. Success requires* only a shift in awareness *in here.*

Forgiveness will release you of the burden that keeps you a prisoner to the past. *"When Thunder and rain set in, the seed pods of all fruits, plants, and trees break open."* The deliverance that results from pardoning mistakes and forgiving misdeeds, allows new life to flourish.

SECTION SIX

Modeling Nature: Principles 41-48

"Untangle the knots; soften the glare."

SUN Decrease

41st Degree: *What is unobservable in the seen world is gestating in unseen form.*

> *"For everything you have missed, you have gained something else;*
> *and for everything you gain, you lose something else."*
>
> *–Emerson*

"Through the sudden release of tension, something is sure to be lost. Hence follows the image of decrease." Just as there is a beginning to the time of flowering, there is also a beginning, which ushers in a time of decline. At the height of summer, autumn is imperceptible and yet summer's decline has already begun. The sage is aware of the moment when phenomena begins to change, and knows *"what ebbs outward flows inward."* When you model nature, you will discover that life's energy remains constant and its economies ensure its continued success. To emulate nature is to be open, productive, and on a continual pathway of evolution.

The idea that "nature abhors a vacuum" comes from the conservation law of physics. It states that the sum total of matter and energy in the universe cannot be destroyed; it can only be transformed. Einstein showed how mass could be converted to and from energy. Accelerator laboratories smash particles through collisions and transform energy into mass. At the same time, energy is transformed back into particles. What is *unobservable* can still exist in unseen form. Decrease is simply part of nature's movement toward rebirth.

The Master's skill in forecasting impending events often made their followers think they were magicians. The great Master had merely followed long enough to trace the outline of change apparent in all transforming phenomena. During winter, life dissipates in the seen world to bring new life to the unseen world below. Decrease is not a negative event, but merely the shifting of life's energy. Whatever is lost in the process paves the way for something else.

It is the natural order of the universe to return to a starting point or cyclical beginning. If something develops to its extreme, it will revert into its opposite condition. Sun is the image of offering something freely in a ceremonial vessel. The unseen potential of Yin becomes accessible when you recognize decrease and prepare for the opportunity of increase. This is how you can romance the unknown and invite it forward. In financial markets too, we see the ebbing and flowing of growth, recession and new growth.

The Master said: *"Things are sometimes increased by being diminished, and at other times are diminished by being added to."* All things are equal from the perspective of growth. Decrease is a prerequisite for increase and new opportunity. We can cut aw. unnecessary growth and the plant grows stronger, while over-watering would destroy it. There are times when decrease or releasing is necessary for healthy growth. Observing the shifting of energy in the natural world, if something is receding in its observable manifestation, it is because unseen energy is gathering somewhere else.

When you *"approach the shape that has no shape,"* you move away from judging experience by the obvious. Someone with riches may have lost their connection to what they value in life. Another faces death and discovers treasure in the type of rebirth that can come from being reconnected to living. Whether it is phenomena transforming energy on the earth, or the closed doors *out there,* which lead to an awakening *in here,* in the great circle energy is always conserved.

The line that separates the inner and outer landscape reveals how *"what ebbs outward flows inward"* and *"what ebbs inward flows outward."* By focusing exclusively on conquest, the inner world can become a wasteland. Too much inner focus and we lose our way. When we disown energy *in here,* it takes shape as an opportunity to discover it *out there.* When we encounter a barrier *out there,* it will give definition to the rising wall *in here*

The conservation of energy can take form in the image of snow on a mountain. During winter, snow is conserved on the hills above, so the snow pack can sustain the population throughout the coming year. The flowing water or energy of future rivers remains in an inanimate condition. This demonstrates how nature does not destroy, but instead, conserves and transforms. Decrease reveals the subtle way that this occurs around you.

"There is nothing constant in the universe. All ebb and flow and every shape that's born, bears in its womb, the seeds of its opposite." To follow the way of nature, when you yield you become strong; when you are strong, you are more able to yield.

The vast majority of life forms are insects and their longevity on this planet suggests that they will outlive us. Their profound ability *to adapt* is what makes life's most fragile creatures it's strongest. The insect world can teach you that life never leads you into crisis; it leads you to become a stronger variation of what you used to be.

When decrease appears, recognize how life turns all things back to fortify them. In this, you will discover abundance and joy by preparing for increase in midst of decrease.

I Increase

42nd Degree: *The law of compensation shows "what is" springs from "what is not."*

"As there is no worldly gain without some loss,
so there is no worldly loss without some gain."

–Francis Quarles

"If decrease goes on and on, it is certain to bring about increase." When the moon's waning has reached its zenith, it begins waxing; when

the sun moves its greatest distance from the earth, it turns back. *"Increase moves gentle and mild; daily progress without limit."* In the Great Circle Increase and Decrease are two aspects of one phenomenon. Because change is universal in all regularly recurring processes of nature, all things will reach a stage where they begin to move toward their opposite condition.

We only give credibility to observable phenomena, although more than 90% of our universe is comprised of the unseen. Scientists explore the "missing mass problem" because they detect gravitational effects on visible matter undetectable by its emitted radiation. Much of the natural world has properties undetectable to the human eye. The sage pays respect to the movement of nature's unseen aspects, to prepare for the opportunity that always arises after a period of decrease. The darkest and most silent hour always comes just prior to the dawn of activity. The void is often frightening, although it is pregnant with enormous possibility.

The law of compensation shows how *"what is, springs from what is not."* A person, who is blind, will develop a more acute way of hearing. Another will compensate for a real or imagined deficiency by overdeveloping other character traits. A cold pressure system in the north will draw warmer weather into the southern regions. Everywhere you look, you will find nature filling in its vacuous spaces to improve "what is not." This constant offers assurance that everything always works out.

In the snowmelt of spring, you can observe stasis transforming into movement. An empty sky can suddenly fill with clouds and rain. You observe events as they happen, but fail to acknowledge the enormous potential of the "unseen" that brought about these events. Increase reveals a lesson about patience, where what appears stationary is merely changing direction. The Master said: *"To the mind that is still, the whole universe surrenders."* The still mind observes how the Way is in a state of perpetual growth.

At the other extreme, we see how "what is not" will spring from "what is." The scarcity of our natural resources reveals the over-depletion that occurs from the discovery of "what is." Someone in denial of self-destructive behavior defends "what is not" in an effort to hide "what is." Insecurity will lead another to over-demonstrate "what is" as a way of protecting "what is not." Anytime you find yourself behaving defensively, you must wonder about the importance of what you are protecting.

Compensation is how energy is transformed at all levels of life. Energy rises, but when it is trapped or repressed, it must take another form. This can happen in a volcano, earthquake, or in the quaking of your inner landscape.

Adaptation is the way nature ensures that "what is" springs from "what is not." New traits emerge when required for survival of a species. Increase and Decrease are natural processions mutually dependent on each other, which cannot be separated. Embracing the unseen cycles of potential Yin allows you to prepare for the successive

Yang that will emerge on the horizon. You can prepare for the sunrise when others see only an empty sky.

KUAI Breakthrough

43rd Degree: *Success comes when you untangle the knots and soften the glare.*

"There is a great deal of unmapped country within us which would have to be taken into account in an explanation of our gusts and storms."

– George Eliot

"When increase goes on unceasingly, there is certain to be a break-through or a resolution." Kuai shows the type of break-through that occurs when a river bursts through a dam and presents two types of scenarios. On one hand, Water opens new pathways through what appeared to be a barrier by virtue of constancy. On the other hand, overcoming obstacles by exerting the will may lead to a pathway of constant battles. Preparing each day for difficulty ensures that you will meet it. Turning inward to re-evaluate the blockage fortifies strength and like Water, you grow in volume and power. Forcing your will on the obstacle will always generate more resistance. You can overcome obstacles by simply recognizing how they fill you with strength.

The resoluteness required to achieve success in activating the power of *te,* must combine vigor with openness. In the image of approaching an obstacle by discrediting it, you can refuse to acknowledge it as having the power to stop you, while acknowledging how it becomes an opportunity to hone you. When you de-anger and emotion, you only validate the *illusion* of a barrier, which wastes your energy. When you *"untangle the knots and soften the glare,"* you eliminate the gusts and storms of the inner landscape. Soften your belief that nature would ever come to obstruct your forward progress; it is always committed to developing the strength of its species. This knowledge leads to a type of Breakthrough.

"The ruler of the South is called Dissatisfaction. The ruler of the North: Revolution. The ruler at the center of the world is Chaos. Dissatisfaction and Revolution met from time to time in the territory of Chaos, and Chaos treated them very hospitably. The two rulers planned how to repay Chaos's kindness. They said: 'Men all have seven holes to their bodies for seeing, hearing, eating and breathing. Our friend here has none of these. Let us try to bore some holes in him.' Each day they bored one hole. On the seventh day Chaos died."

The chaos created by exerting your will and ignoring life's fundamental benevolence will dissipate when you untangle your beliefs and soften your defensive tendencies. All you believe will eventually come to meet you as *"the Way goes round and round."* Transforming the energy of emotion into an inner shifting of suppleness will always lead to wellness, balance and success.

KOU Coming to Meet

44th Degree: *Hope is like a flower forced to grow without sunlight.*

"Most of the shadows of this life are caused by
standing in one's own sunshine."
– Emerson

"Through resoluteness, one is certain to encounter something. Hence, follows the principle of coming to meet." Kou embodies how you waste much energy fighting against imaginary foes. *"Riding and hunting make the mind go wild with excitement."* Expecting difficulty can be a way of ensuring that you meet with constant difficultly.

"Some things are distinctions made by the senses, others are distinctions made by the mind. Discard the one and you will lay hold of the other." When you discard judgment, you return to a more innocent way of observing the world around you.

Resoluteness can sometimes cost you *"your inner treasure"* that remains at home with the possibilities of the unknown. The Master said: *"To know, yet to think one does not know is best."*

A student asked: *"If nature creates all things, then is evil too, its creation?"*

The Master replied: *"What need has nature of thought and care? When the sun goes, the moon comes; when the moon goes, the sun comes. Sun and moon alternate, thus light comes into view. When cold goes, heat comes; when heat goes, cold comes. Can one be any different from the other? Suchness is neither pure nor impure."*

"What is the reason for the cruelty in the world?" The student continued: *"What cause has nature for crime and suffering?"*

"In the absence of seeing, you wander in the darkness in search of light," the Master replied. *"Yet, darkness comes every night without fail. One who excels in understanding uses no counting rods. Why struggle like beating a drum in search of a fugitive?"*

Using no counting rods or placing unnatural judgments upon what you see allows you to recognize the purposefulness of nature. If you think of yourself as a victim and blame the outside world for your condition, you might never discover life's fundamental goodness. To *"beat a drum in search of a fugitive,"* is to attract others that can share in your misery. Fugitives will come, but you will meet others who are *also hiding.*

Psychologists agree that people who commit atrocities are conflicted by inner compulsions. Coming To Meet reveals how you confuse *searching* with experience, while you beat your drum to attract all that you believe. A hardened perspective will be made pliable. *"When the people lack a proper sense of awe, it seems that an awful visitation descends on them."* Thwarting change with illogical absolutes and experience comes to carve away your shackles. Coming to meet is how you create your own misfortune and opportunity for freedom at the same time.

"Thus the good transforms the bad, and the bad is the material that the good works on. Not to value the teacher, nor to love the material, betrays great bewilderment."

Our idea of opposites gives contrasting symbolism meaning: up/down, sound/silence, and order/disorder. Although they stand in relationship to define one another, they fail to capture the real essence of *what is.* One variation is simply a degree of the other and therefore, *"suchness is neither pure nor impure."* The image that would appear in the middle of each word is the uncarved block. You may find attachment in the things that generate a response in you, when in reality the actual value resides in *your response.* Once you have been moved by the experience or the *"carved block,"* let it go.

The Master was having tea with two students, tossed his fan to one of them and asked, *"What is this?"* The student opened it and began fanning himself. The Master nodded because the student had transcended the need to give the object a name.

"Now you," he passed the fan to the other student. This one closed it and began scratching his neck with it. He opened it, and placed a piece of cake on it, offering it to the Master. Beyond the need to classify the present in terms of the past, real vision begins. Look beyond the limitations you place on experience to return to simplicity.

Walking around knowing *"when there is frost underfoot, solid ice is not far off,"* you tread with care, because the first sign of danger makes you defensive. Yet, there is a fine line between avoiding danger and stalking adversity. Danger is often the first phase of *emerging opportunity. "The more taboos there are in the empire, the poorer the people. The conflict between right and wrong is the sickness of the mind."* Hope is like a flower forced to grow without sunlight. Hope is a blindfold, which keeps you from discovering the beauty of *what is.*

Kou is the image of intercourse and how you can be made whole by integrating *that thing* which is completely opposite from everything you believe about yourself. Kou demonstrates both the danger and opportunity presented when opposites first approach each other. The great image of what you believe will eventually come to meet you. *"Coming to you and meeting with no harm, it will be safe and sound."*

When you observe, reflect, and recognize how each experience is a reflection of your inner empire, you come to recognize the profound harmony at the root of life.

TS'UI Gathering Together

45th Degree: *Success is allowing your lot to reach its highest degree.*

"It is while you are patiently toiling at the little tasks of life
that the meaning and shape
of the great whole of life dawns on you."

– Phillips Brooks

"When creatures meet one another, they mass together. Hence, follows the principle of gathering together." Over the Earth, is the Joyous Lake in the image of crowds drawing together. *"The strong stands in the middle, therefore others mass around it."* The nuclear trigrams suggest a character that emulates the movement and influence of the Wind, while remaining steadfast like a Mountain.

"When you have in your hold the great image, the empire will come to you."

The mind forever travels in search of success to be achieved *out there.* Yet, to be still, while *"in silent harmony with one's ultimate capacity, means allowing one's lot to reach its highest degree."* Like water growing in volume, use each moment as an opportunity to blossom. The Master said: *"Nothing exists but the present. If one cannot live there, one cannot live anywhere."*

You must not make *where you are going* more important than *where you are. "If one allows their nature to follow its own course, there will be no place for joy and sorrow."*

"Only when you stop liking and disliking will all be understood." Your journey is not in the pursuit of perfection; seek only the authenticity that unfurls from within. Like the performer who discovers that self-consciousness is a barrier to their craft, being authentically natural is what makes you attractive. *"This is why the sage puts themselves last and finds that they are in the forefront; treats the self as extraneous and it is preserved. Is it not because one is without personal desires that one is able to fulfill one's desires?"*

Te is not a virtue that develops from moral rectitude; it is the creative power of authenticity that comes from spontaneous and natural expression. If your character is authentic, you become quite naturally effective. *"Because this power is most true, within it there is confidence."* This confidence creates the magnetism that draws others to you.

Ts'ui is the image of grass growing and multiplying We observe how life drives the strength of the individual root through interdependency. Its strength then relies upon the growing strength of the collective root, while the collective thrives on the power of the individual. You may gather in places because of the ways that you are like others, but your te is revealed in the ways *that you are different.* This contrast allows you to hear your drummer on the pathway to your destiny.

When you are authentic in the moment, you can detect the greater shape and the larger meaning of life's interdependency. *"That is why the sage concentrates on the core of things and not the husk. They let go of the 'that' to lay hold of the 'this."* When you remove the outer covering that brings you together with others, you discover that *this* is the core of who you really are.

In life, you participate in groups and serve others with your unique way of giving. In this way, you are not taking but giving; through giving, you will learn more about yourself.

SHENG Pushing Upward

46th Degree: *If you pay respect to the great, you pave the way for your own greatness.*

"It is always better to fail in doing something
than to excel in doing nothing."

– Chinese Proverb

"Massing toward the top is called pushing upward. That which pushes upward does not come back." We sometimes believe successful people get a lucky break, but more often than not, it was the heaping up of small efforts that led to their success. You can be successful, but if your success came at the expense of your authenticity, it will leave you feeling empty.

When you model nature, you will see the progression of how big things have their beginnings in the small. In the atom, molecule, cells, tissues, organs, people or nations, big things emerge from the heaping up of small things. To create a type of success that generates fulfillment, the sage builds the foundation from *the inside - out.*

The Gentle Wind is the constancy of wood that pushes upward through the Earth, and Sheng is the image of something growing with an emphasis on expansion. *"One generation plants trees; another gets the shade. What grows upward does not come back"* because the flowering usually occurs much later than the actual effort.

The Master said: *"In time, you carry on your back, the Yin; In time, you embrace in your arms, the Yang."* This captures the idea of how you carry on with your efforts, even while the results may not be apparent. Ascending vertically suggests the rise from obscurity to a position of power because of your sincerity. *"One who pays respect to the great paves the way for one's own greatness."* You tend to the small with the knowledge that everything is a part of the great whole.

When work displays immediate results, you are gratified, but because you cannot see the result, you may question what you are doing. To *"shine and not dazzle"* is the sense of holding to your sense of inner purpose, without the need for recognition. Only you know the importance of what you are doing. *If it is real, it will endure.* All effort is consequential because even small contributions are important. Like the principle of waiting, there is no immediate response. Sincerity strengthens when you do the small things that make you qualified to do even greater things.

Through convergence, you stand in the collective to find your core. Pushing upward alone, you achieve success through perseverance. Thus, you can transform the devotion of following your inner drummer or te into greatness.

There are many cases where executive leadership in major corporations rises from the mailroom. To achieve great things, do not measure your efforts in terms of big and small; *all* effort is meaningful. Like the Gentle and penetrating Wind, if you consistently do even the smallest of things, you will ascend. Without obvious results, you can understand a deeper meaning of gratification: *it is your devotion to the work that makes you great.*

K'UN Oppression

47th Degree: *Success is a pathway of self-completion and the seed is always within you.*

"Perfection is reached, not when there is no longer anything to add,
but when there is no longer anything to take away."

– Antoine de St. Exupery

"If one pushes upward without stopping, there is sure to be oppression. Hence, follows the principle of oppression and exhaustion." The Joyous Lake is dispersing water into the Abysmal Water below. Since both bodies of water tend to move downward, eventually the Lake is drained. We are told, *"there is no water in the Lake"* and when oppression appears, you can lose your joy and consider giving up.

The Lake represents an attempt to contain fulfillment, while the Abysmal Water suggests an inexhaustible source. K'un's message is that while you tend to attach yourself to what can be held within the hand, you cannot know today what will come to fulfill you tomorrow. Like an ocean that cannot be depleted, because all streams lead back to it, you access a source within that is inexhaustible. It is inexhaustible only when you do not try to contain it.

When you model nature, observe how all life forms follow their instincts or an inborn pattern of development. Adaptation reveals how oppression *out there* acts as a mechanism to unleash your capabilities *in here*. To measure success only by outward accomplishment, you may fail to see how adversity pushes you back to discover your real capabilities. When you explore your value in the mirror of the unknown, you are "just so," and living the life you are meant to be living here and now.

Oppression pushes back against you to whittle away the unnecessary that would have led to exhaustion, until only the necessary remains. The Master said: *"When great responsibility is about to befall one, life appears to confound all undertakings. Thereby it stimulates the mind, toughens the nature and improves all deficiencies."* Without friction or the natural tension of life, the unnecessary cannot be carved away. Being whittled to perfection demonstrates how *"great fullness seems empty."*

Believing that life is working against you always leads to exhaustion. Success comes when you can approach experience without prejudice. *"With gentle compassion, I can be brave. With economy, I can be liberal. Not presuming to claim precedence in the world I can make myself a vessel fit for the most distinguished service."* In the image of a tree growing within an enclosure, you can be hemmed in and still grow. Success takes root when *"you are abundant and yet, not reactive."*

Bamboo symbolizes great virtue because as its leaves droop, it portrays how one can bow down to the changes and still be content. When the winds of change blow, it moves too, and simply bends in shimmering laughter. You will achieve great fullness when you recognize success is a pathway of self-completion, and that the seed is always within. *"The power that is most sufficient looks inadequate."*

When you do not contend with the nature of things, nothing contends with you. Real power grows. When there is no longer anything to be removed, you are rich.

CHING The Well

48th Degree: *You can spend a lifetime and still never come anywh... exhausting the resources that are inside of you.*

"Your vision will become clear only when you can look into your own heart. Who looks outside, dreams; who looks within, awakes."

– Carl Jung

"One that is oppressed above is sure to turn downward. Hence follows the idea of the Well." When oppressed outwardly, you eventually turn inward. *"The town may be changed but the Well cannot be changed."* Circumstances change, although the root of experience always leads to the same place: *within*. You can change what your experiences will *"look and feel like"* by traveling inward to look at life's reflection in the great reservoir of your heart.

The Master said: *"That is why the sage is concerned with what is inside and not what is seen outside. One abandons the 'that' to lay hold of the 'this.'"* The difference between *this* and *that* is ownership.

This resides in the Well, and Ching is the image of accessing the unknown depths of your mysterious nature. The Gentle symbolizes wood, and how a plant stalk finds nourishment from the wellspring beneath the earth. *"Discover the Well before you are thirsty."* As a principle that models nature, you can access this inexhaustible resource within to find your unique pattern of development. You could spend a lifetime and never come anywhere close to exhausting its resources.

Ching is the state of mind that bubbles from the great reservoir of te by being just so. In the image of nine fields with the well at the center, each family farmed their individual fields, but collectively worked the ninth field at the center, since it housed the well and belonged to the lord. The eight fields represent their daily routine, but the ninth field required a *sacrifice* if one would draw from the Well. To access your undiscovered potential you need to sacrifice the known and travel into a strange territory.

The Master said: *"Penetrating under the water and bringing up the water: this is the Well. If one goes down almost to the water and the rope does not go all the way, one has not achieved anything."* You must discover this pathway, and reach this inner sustenance before you are thirsty.

Symbolically, water has always personified the unseen and unknown. In dreams, it embodies how we approach change, and its behavior reflects how we feel about these changes. It reflects our inner well-being and the reservoir of what remains unconscious. Many myths present water as the powerful reservoir, where the hero must solve a mystery before receiving a great treasure from its depths. The Abysmal appears dangerous only to those afraid to test their inner depths.

The Well holds the unseen or unrecognized potential you can draw upon as power. *"Look within and discover the world; look without and discover the self;"* the inner and outer cannot be separated. *"The Well shows the field of character, abiding in its place, yet it has an influence on other things."* Any changes to what you experience *out there* must first be cultivated *in here*. Whatever remains hidden is actively seeking expression and experience always brings it forward.

When you look into your heart, you discover sincerity. Composure within will always reflects itself on experience. This is the rope that goes all the way down to the water. When you are sincere, you discover a way within. When you access the Well, you find the pathway from your center outward. You can draw upon a treasure that cannot be exhausted.

SECTION SEVEN

The Land of Te: Principles 49-56

"In the landscape of spring, there is neither high nor low."

KO Molting/Revolution

49th Degree: *Unhappiness is the first sign that something powerful stirs within you.*

"A mind once stretched by a new idea
never regains its original dimension."

– Oliver Wendell Holmes

"The setup of a well must necessarily be revolutionized in the course of time. Hence, follows the idea of revolution. Revolution means the removal of what has become antiquated." The Well connects you to your inner direction or te, although molting is how your real nature is coaxed forward to skin awareness. In the way that animals molt in the natural world, it is instinctual and necessary. Over time, the waters of the Well must flow clear to keep its contents purified.

Long ago, we used ropes and buckets, while the Well remained at the center of all social interchanges. Today, we simply turn on a faucet and barely speak to each other. Experience will always have more meaning when life revolves around the inner Well. Old ways of detaching from experience will no longer work and a revolution in how you approach experience is required.

"In the landscape of spring, there is neither high nor low" because during spring, everything is in a state of *becoming*. Shedding the old skin allows you to express your full potential. Fear, or the need to conform, will keep you from natural expression; *only you can know what it means to be fearlessly yourself.* As a principle that takes you into the land of te, you make a commitment to move forward from your center.

Ko is the image of an animal skin stretched on a frame. You can work your hide, or outer covering to make it applicable to the present. Shedding the skin of the past, you are made ready for your debut. Molting is how animals renew their outer covering as the seasons change.

Like an animal, you can fearfully take on the appearance of the landscape through conformity to hide your real self. You have a tendency to remain faceless in a crowd, although as you molt, your individuality comes to skin awareness. During the season of rebirth, you will discover that unhappiness is the hunger pain for change: it is the first sign that something powerful is stirring within you. Whereas the old way of approaching experience allowed you to remain hidden, you must peel away the layers that hide your real nature.

Being self-actualized and spontaneously yourself is the only way that you can remain connected to life. When civilization held mysticism and religion above reason, the world grew dark. Turning back to appreciate nature, they circumnavigated the globe, and discovered that the world was indeed, round. The Great Turning always creates balance. The Master said: *"The One unites the duality of Two."* Beyond the two, is the image of any unnatural condition, and a lack of balance that generates the turning.

When you separate yourself from life, you create two ways of viewing the world. *"This* is who I really am, but *that* is what the world expects me to be." Somewhere in the middle of 'this' and 'that,' your real life has taken on a protective covering. To prepare for your revolution, shed your protective skin. You will discover that *this* is the person you were meant to be and you must cherish bringing it forward.

TING The Cauldron

50th Degree: *You hold the power to become the master of your existence.*

"Everyone is a moon, and has a dark side,

which he never shows anyone."

– Mark Twain

"Nothing transforms things so much as the ting. Therefore follows the idea of a cauldron." The ting was cast of bronze, with three legs and two carrying rings on each side. Like most cauldrons, it served ritual food and acted as a vessel for sacrifices to the unseen higher beings. A ritual is how you validate the unknown, unseen or unspoken through ceremony. On a mundane level, you tip your hat, shake hands, or kiss on the cheek as each culture prescribes. This leads to habitual behavior, which becomes common within the empire. Doing something

habitually instead of authentically is how the inner empire can become a wasteland.

"Inner and outer, it matters not" they cannot be separated. Famine within will always project itself upon the outer world. When you do *what is expected* of you, authenticity is lost and famine grows within and without. The Cauldron suggests approaching the invisible with reverence and a sense of sacrifice. The Well is the source within, but the Cauldron reflects how this inner source nourishes you like food. The work you do to transform the landscape *in here* will be powerfully reflected upon events *out there.* This is how the sage becomes the master of their experiences. In this, there is sustenance.

The Gentle Wind now becomes the wood used to inspire the fiery flame beneath the Cauldron. Unlike the image of the Well, which uses the Wood to draw from the Abysmal Water, the Wood now gives life to and feeds the Fire of transformation. The Cauldron ripens you for your debut.

The nuclear trigram of the Gentle Wind seeks upward penetration, while the Creative remains firm at the center. It captures the image of how you are gathered toward the center of te, where *"thirty spokes share one hub."* At its rim, you surface to call experience fortune or fate in the random turning of events. Events are not random, in that what is full becomes empty; what is still begins to stir as the Way goes round and round.

Connected to te, where the center of the wheel moves the least, you are no longer buffeted by outer events. You have no need to travel in circles, reacting to each event, as if you are not connected to it. Everything you will ever become takes root from the center of your te. Yet, sometimes you must traverse the wasteland within to resurrect its voice.

Exploring the power of your inner drummer, you will find a meaningful pattern unfolding in daily events to exercise your growing power. The Clinging suggest an awareness of the synergy existing between the inner empire, and how it takes shape in the outer world. Like the incense and smoke burned during spiritual offerings, the flame brings the visible to meet the invisible. At the same time, approaching the invisible can shed light on the visible.

Observing experience, you may fail to see how it mirrors the unseen world within. As the seen and unseen interact, what is called fate is the way in which life moves to unleash your real nature. You must question what you hold to be sacred, and learn to let it go. In a world of change, the idea of sacred holds little relevance.

The Master said: *"At dusk, the cock announces dawn; at midnight, the bright sun."* What is visible in one realm is only a portion of what remains unseen in another. Transcending any sense of boundaries, the Cauldron becomes a ritual vessel that offers you a deeper understanding of how you are nourished by life. Nature always responds to lead you back to the center of your te.

CHEN Shocking

51st Degree: *Success comes when you can achieve tranquility in disturbance.*

"The gem cannot be polished without friction,

nor man perfected without trials."

– Confucius

"Among the custodians of the sacred vessel, the oldest son comes first. Hence, follows the idea of the Arousing or shocking Thunder." Chen was personified as the oldest son who holds a prominent position within the family. Without the freedom to keep growing, the Arousing portrays movement that disengages you from complacency. *"Shock brings success. Shock comes – oh oh! Laughing words – ha ha!"* Like a clap of thunder, sudden and spontaneous events ensue where you will observe how *"that which goes against the Way comes to an early end."*

"The shock terrifies for a hundred miles, although one does not let fall the sacrificial spoon and chalice." The sacrificial spoon and chalice carry the idea of the Well and Cauldron as the utensils used for transformation. In the Thunder and rain, we see how nature's chain of events leads to subtle transformation. What ensues is a chain reaction because the atmosphere has become unproductive. When you are stuck in a transformational process, Shocking events come to release you from stagnation, but do not forget that you hold the key and the power to transform.

The Master said: *"Everything is in destruction; everything is in construction. This is called tranquility in disturbance. Tranquility in disturbance means perfection."* Tranquility in disturbance comes when you recognize that whatever takes form in necessary. It is just so. *"The shock terrifies and fear brings good fortune."* Fear has little purpose other than being the reaction of one fighting against the changes. On a pathway to authenticity, fear is aroused from slumber so that it can be transformed into productive power and *the freedom to move.* Understanding the necessity of what transpires; fear and trembling give way to tranquility and faith in the way.

In the natural world, a baby albatross will leave the comfort and safety of its nest on an island. Before it can fly, it must venture into the ocean like a duck, paddling to achieve the momentum necessary for flight. At the same time, tiger sharks will swarm in the shallows, seeking their opportunity for sustenance. The albatross that is frightened enough to attempt what it has never tried before, *will fly.* Like the baby albatross that learns to fly, that part of you that has remained dormant will resurface in the image of quaking and excited rain.

The shocking always comes as the event necessary to transform fear into new life: it is fundamental to your survival. *"Nothing is worse than struggling not to give play to feelings one cannot control. This is called the Double Injury and of those who sustain it, none live out their natural span."* Doctors agree that stress is the silent killer, yet stress can be viewed as productive energy that is coming to the surface to be transformed.

Closing down, stagnation and fear can turn energy back on the body. The shocking is the good fortune that awakens you to self-destructive tendencies. Holding yourself in contempt for harboring natural urges, you may intellectualize taboos that go against your base nature. In proportion to how critical you have become of others, you will recognize the severity of your inner critic. When you believe others are judging you, turn within to see how you judge yourself.

"Precious things lead one astray. A situation only becomes favorable when one adapts to it. The kind man discovers it and calls it kind. The wise man discovers it and calls it wise. The people use it day by day and are unaware of it." Even the most shocking situations embody life's movement toward renewal. Whatever is removed makes room for something meaningful to grow in its place.

As the image of an earthquake, the ground gives way to loosen what you held to be solid and precious. You can bend like bamboo, yielding with laughter in the winds of renewal. Whatever the event, you are released of the structures that have become the tower and prison of your real nature.

KEN Keeping Still

52nd Degree: *You will discover the germinating power of te in the silence where a thousand seeds are becoming the landscape of spring.*

"As soon as man does not take his existence for granted, but beholds it as something unfathomably mysterious, thought begins."

– Albert Schweitzer

"Things cannot move continuously and one must make them stop. Therefore follows the image of keeping still. Keeping the back still, one no longer feels the body." Just as the back is a part of the body, which remains invisible to us, the Master said: *"Going into the courtyard, the king does not see the people."* Turning within, you must sometimes disengage yourself from outer events to re-connect with your power. *"Composure will straighten out your inner life"* and reflect itself upon experience.

There are times to advance forward and times to keep still. Ken is the image of two Mountains facing each other so the inner and outer can meet in meditation. *"One does not permit the thoughts to go beyond the situation."* No longer distracted by sensory input and expectation, you can reconnect with the voice of sincerity within. In the image of an eye, looking around to see what has led to the present situation, when you lose your sense of stillness; you lose the self and become lost in your surroundings. *"To find the self, you need only recapture your sense of stillness."*

When the Master asked a pupil why he would sit in meditation, the pupil replied that it was a way to know Tao. The Master picked up a tile and began to polish it against a rock. When the pupil asked why he did this, the Master replied it was a way to make a mirror.

The pupil asked: *"How could polishing a tile make a mirror?"* The Master replied: *"How could sitting in meditation produce Tao?"*

You turn inward to reflect on events, where the inner and outer can meet in meditation; not to deny the relevance of all experience. Unlike other types of meditation, the ancient Taoist sought only to release the sense of separation existing between *in here* and *out there.*

Ken is a message about recapturing a pure perspective, in the image of birds moving through the sky. Birds seek their destiny, but leave no trace; they are challenged by circumstances, yet eagerly celebrate each sunrise. *"Continue easy and you are right."*

The Master said: *"When the fish is caught the trap is forgotten. You gallop around in search of the mind and are unable to stop it."* When the idea comes, the mind is forgotten. Yet, the mind is the trap, while what you capture is the "carved block" that merely represents your passing desires. No mind allows you to appreciate a greater movement that is endless. Life speaks to you and you must cherish each opportunity to understand it.

"The fish must not be allowed to leave the deep." The fish is the treasure of te. It is that place within, which holds you to the center of each experience. Cultivate an awareness that remains unattached, deep and therefore, becomes profoundly powerful.

The Master asked: *"Where is your place of birth?"*

The pupil replied: *"This morning I ate rice and now I am hungry again."* Need is an endless movement without a home.

The Master asked: *"How is my hand like Tao?"* The pupil replied: *"Playing the lute under the moon."* Joy comes from tracing the outline of your real nature unfolding upon the tapestry of life.

The Master asked: *"How is my foot like a donkey's foot?"*

"When the white heron stands upon the snow, it has a different color." All things remain relative to each other…that is all you can really know.

When you shadow Tao, it shadows your beliefs. Beliefs become traps on the pathway of true perception. Whatever the trap, you can unseat it by letting go.

"The court is corrupt. The fields are overgrown with weeds. The granaries are empty, yet there are those, who are dressed in fineries." Oblivious to a lifeless inner landscape, you may come to wear the costume of what is expected of you. If you can open to the mystery within, the real journey of individuation begins.

CHIEN Development

53rd Degree: *Success comes when you can pull your nature forward rather than pushing yourself into the world.*

"A man will be imprisoned in a room with a door that's unlocked
and opens inwards, as long as it does not
occur to him to pull rather than push."

– Ludwig Wittgenstein

"Things cannot stop forever; therefore follows the idea of development." The Gentle Wind moves over the Mountain portraying the image of a tree developing according to the laws of its being. The tree on a mountain benefits all, but must grow slowly in accordance with the seasons. The seed holds within, all that it will one day become, although it must remain steadfast through the changing climate.

As the sage moves forward from the foundation of *te*, the tree becomes a lesson about perseverance and patience in its unfolding. Because its growth is slow and steady, it demonstrates the principle: *"a little then benefited; a lot then perplexed."* If it shoots up too quickly, or at the wrong time, its roots will never keep it upright when the first storms set in. The development and expression of *te* must be cultivated slowly and patiently.

Bo Ju ji wrote about trees: *"they are useful friends to me and they fulfill my wish for conversations with the wise."* Steadfast and benefiting those seeking comfort, they were celebrated as the wisest of the earth's teachers. *"When difficulties come, do not lose sight of the power of life. It is only in the depth of winter when there is frost and snow that we have means of knowing how luxuriant the pines and cypresses are. To be in unbroken contact with the stem of life, the germinating power of nature, and to make te the door to all wisdom; that is what is meant by being a sage."*

You may push outward to seek success, although if you pulled yourself forward from the roots of the unseen kingdom within, you will find it. No two trees are alike and they do not grow well in each other's shadow. *"Only one that is entirely real in each experience will have the power to give full development to one's nature. Realness is self-completing and the Way is self-directing. Realness is the end as well as the beginning of things, for without realness there would be no things at all; which is why the sage prizes above everything coming-to-be-real."* Captured in the image of a tree, development is a combination of self-direction and sustenance that comes from our root. The changes in the climate around us steward our rebirth.

Development is the gradual way that you cultivate the roots of who you are, rather than outwardly searching for acceptance. When you merely strive to be real, success will come naturally. Emulating the tree, remain steadfast in your unbroken contact with the germinating power of life.

KUEI MEI Subordinate

54th Degree: *Instinct is the bubbling of te, excited by the prospect of your coming-to-be-real.*

"Not the cry, but the flight of the wild duck,
leads the flock to fly and follow."
– Chinese Proverb

"Through progress, one is sure to reach the place, where one belongs. Hence follows the idea of the subordinate." The Arousing Thunder moves over the Joyous Lake, while the nuclear trigrams reveal the connection to something profound stirring within. Before moving forward, Kuei Mei is a lesson of *"understanding the transitory in the light of the eternity at*

the end." Some things change, while other aspects remain enduring. Some things lead, while others follow. Like the marriage of man and wife, they are brought together by something other than logic. By following only heart and instinct, they discover a life of fulfillment.

An artist understands the idea of following completely. *"Once there was a wood carver. When he first began to carve, he gazed at the wood in front of him. After three years, he no longer saw it as a piece of wood, but as something of shape that merely required the carving necessary to give it form. In time, he no longer saw it with the eyes, but apprehended it with a different type of vision. Decision and action were simultaneously joined, and as he worked, his sense organs were always in abeyance. By conforming to the structure that led him, he carved deftly and without effort. He said: 'Where part meets part, there is always space, and a knife blade has no thickness. Insert an instrument that has no thickness into a structure that is amply spaced and surely, the work is effortless.'"*

Like the woodcarver, your te is given shape by experience. Your pathway is "amply spaced" and when you "have no thickness," you are open to releasing what keeps it hidden. When you struggle against your nature, you meet the unchangeable laws of existence and the unalterable tendencies within. When you subordinate yourself to life, you will discover that *"the greatest cutting does not sever."* Life merely carves away what keeps you from following your nature.

At the same time, you can approach experience like an artist who knows the shape of what is to come, and simply removes what is blocking its expression. Undaunted by the pieces of "carved block" that fall by the wayside, the artist is completely connected to inner vision. The more this inner vision is respected, the more pronounced it becomes.

The migrating bird does not follow the cry of other birds. Each bird follows its own instinctual call to fly. Although you follow the shape of what you want your future to become, it is given further definition in the mirror of what unfolds right now. More often than not, the result is more than we expected.

The Master said: *"To understand the transitory in the eternity at the end, release the experience and hold only to the thread."* This will allow you to open to the instinctual pull of your evolutionary journey.

"Go on to the limit of emptiness: hold fast to the stability of stillness. For, all things were made by one process and they all turn back. They may flourish abundantly, but each turns and goes home to the root from which it came. Therefore, to turn back is to reclaim your destiny." When you make peace with life, you will discover its enormous power to guide you. As if something already knows your shape, experience carves away only the layers that keep you from coming-to-be-real.

FENG Zenith

55th Degree: *If you make your heart like a lake, life will continuously fulfill you.*

"Everything flows and nothing abides;
everything gives way and nothing stays fixed."
– *Heraclitus*

"That which attains the place in which it belongs is sure to become great. Therefore follows the idea of abundance." In the land of te, you can operate from scarcity or abundance. Scarcity is a kingdom in which all of the people are hungry because they do not know how to grow sustenance. They take what they feel is missing, and conquer others out of a sense of inadequacy. Operating from a place of scarcity ensures that you will discover opportunities to validate its existence.

Abundance is a kingdom with a horn of plenty, where the people cultivate and share in the knowledge of an inexhaustible source. Described as the Land of Te or virtue, *"they know how to make things but do not hoard. They give but seek no return."*

Feng is the zenith of abundance, where something is so full that it overflows. These overflowing inner reserves show how you are not made empty even while you give; this is the way of a kingdom of abundance. The Master said: *"When the sun stands at midday, it begins to set: be not sad. The fullness and emptiness of life wax and wane in the course of time."* If you make your heart like a lake, life will always fulfill you.

"The wise stand firm and do not change direction," and just as *"a gusty wind and downpour cannot last all day,"* the changing climate always brings sustenance to the garden within. The arrival of the longest day of the year means tomorrow ushers in decline. Yet, when the days are darker, we spend more time with family, celebrating the ways in which we are thankful.

Like all of the things of the earth, after abundance, you turn inward to regenerate for the coming year and make resolutions that will lead to wellness. Abundance can only endure through gentle dispersion, or by letting go of what you cling to; what is disbursed will always leave room so that you can be re-filled.

When you engage in the constant action of conquering others to fill a sense of inadequacy, you invite conflict. *"In conflict, it is love that wins. Love is the strongest protection. If you have love, it feels as if Heaven itself is keeping you safe. Make your heart like a lake, with calm, still surface and great depths of kindness."*

Although the sun appears to set and the moon appears to wane, they always remain full. Life always moves to fill you, but if you are un-fulfilled, you may fill yourself with the unnecessary. All you protect gives rise to what you will encounter. *"Too much holding onto anything will leave you perplexed. Leave your kingdom and its ways; take nature as your guide and travel to the land of Te."*

LU The Wanderer

56th Degree: *And the still deeper secret of the secret: the land that is nowhere, that is your true home.*

"He had the uneasy manner of a man who is not among his own kind,
and who has not seen enough of the world to feel
that all people are in some sense his own kind."

– Willa Cather

"Whatever greatness may exhaust itself upon, this much is certain: it loses a home. Hence follows the idea of the wanderer." You can listen to the

words of a Wanderer, mastering the art of living in a place without boundaries: *"This is the deeper secret of the secret. The land that is nowhere, that is the true home. When some people travel, they merely contemplate what is before their eyes; when I travel I contemplate mutability."*

When you wander in the land of te, you master a vessel in a world of discovery. You push onward toward new horizons because *"the greatest traveler does not know where he is going."* In the land of te, there are no limits to what you might become.

When far from home, you take your inner treasure and ritual along. *"When the heart is uneasy, we support it with ritual."* Your daily ritual is more obvious when you must pack it for a long journey. When you travel with companions, much energy is wasted in fortifying the dynamics of familiar routines. When you are traveling alone, you are closer to te, because you are free to be yourself.

Some part of you is active during dreaming, where you access an awareness that becomes a postcard sent to awaken the sleeping one below. Each night, you travel back and forth from a strange land to understand the real essence of who you might become. If the Land of Te could be defined, it would resemble the dreamscape. When you dream, you access a place *"as though there is no home to go back to."* When morning comes, you travel *"across the doorsill where the two worlds touch."* In daily life, you can also travel across a tapestry that transcends boundaries.

In the image of people loyal to a home that is far away, the Wanderer points to an endless expanse of sky, and shows you that the horizon is an illusion and there are no real boundaries to your capabilities. The seed of self-realization is unfolding regardless of where you are. The present does not linger, and as you travel onward, you develop a sense of loyalty to your center. Everywhere you go, there you are, in a subtle demonstration of your unfolding.

To approach the mystery of Tao, *"you cannot take hold of it, but you cannot lose it. In not being able to get it, you get it. When you are silent, it speaks; when you speak, it is silent. The great gate is wide open to bestow alms, and no crowd is blocking the way."* When you discover the great gate, you may lose a paradigm, but will discover your true home.

SECTION EIGHT

Accessing the Great Power of Nature: Principles 57-64

"One who never fails always succeeds."

SUN Penetrating Wind

57th Degree: *Something very profound is also committed to your success.*

"When the oak is felled the whole forest echoes with its fall,

but a hundred acorns are sown in silence by an unnoticed breeze."

– Thomas Carlyle

"As a wanderer, there is nothing that might receive you. Therefore follows the idea of the Gentle and penetrating Wind." Success means more than material wealth; it is the peace, which comes from knowing you have made the right decisions. Yet, the idea of making choices allows you to get lost in the illusion of good and bad. Instead, you can make the choice to follow life on its terms.

In an instant, life can suddenly become meaningful and you may feel that something profound is happening. Yet, you must ask yourself what transpired in your life in that moment that made you open to its ways? Life is always touching you in sublime ways, although you sometimes only glimpse it when circumstances emerge to *slow you down*. Observing the transformative power of nature as it guides its creatures, this power within you and its connection to everything around you will always defeat your efforts to imagine how potent it really is.

The sublimity of life demonstrates wisdom that continuously wrestles you back to yourself. When you stop trying to comprehend life in your terms, you can open to understanding yourself in its terms: *there is something undeniably unique about you and its potential knows no bounds.* Nature always fortifies the strengths of its successful variations. At the same time, it weeds away what does not work or what may lead to stagnation. Either way it is committed to your success.

You are one of its many diversities; no better, but certainly every bit as important as the purposeful creatures you observe around you. Life gently prods each creature to be whatever it designed it to be; at the same time, it allows for variation. Rather than search for direction *out there,* awaken to life's evolutionary thrust *in here*. *"Be open; that is all."*

Develop your character to match the wisdom of nature: *"it attracts, but does not summon."* Nature's successes are the result of the freedoms it allows each species. Just as the bee and the flower sustain each other, sustenance is the result of attraction, interdependency and necessity. Trust that you receive just what you need to thrive.

"The Gentle shows the exercise of character. One can weigh things and remain hidden." Without *doing* anything, you can influence the outside world and gain control over what unfolds. If you do not hoard, nothing will be undone. *"Be open, that is all."*

The Master said: *"What is easy attracts the easy; what is hard will attract the hard."* If you are open, there is no need for life to break away your hardness. If you remain easy, you invite the easy.

This is how you can gently influence events. Success comes when you no longer *"contend and yet are be able to conquer; do not declare your will and yet, get a response; do not summon, and still have things come spontaneously to you."* Te, as the "power in me," when tapped as the same energy that drives nature toward individuation, does not fight the very thing that gives it expression. When you are "just so" all that you need always comes spontaneously to you. If you want more, *"remain empty"* or find ways of sharing what you have.

Steadfast and open, *"life leads the thoughtful person on a path of many windings. Now the course is checked, now it runs straight again."* In the image of items arranged on a table, something is needed to support them. After each experience, you will discover how life supports you to roam free. Moving effortlessly like the Wind, you can have a sense of contentment where others experience frustration. Adjusting your sails to harness the winds of life that guide you, "one who never fails" is the mark of one devoted to the Way.

Penetrating experience with the same effort as the gentle Wind, you will discover *"when the decision is made, all things come to you."* Embracing nature's pursuit of the best of what it might become, you awaken into a world that always meets you half way to bring it forward.

TUI Joy

58th Degree: *If you never fail, you will always succeed.*

> *"If you would hit the mark, you must aim a little above it;*
> *every arrow that flies, feels the attraction of the earth."*
> – *Longfellow*

"Once you have penetrated something, you rejoice." When experience is no longer separated by *in here* and *out there,* you discover a profound power that allows you to be *"active everywhere, but are not carried away; in your knowledge of grace, you are free of care. Content in your circumstances and genuine in kindness, you are the expression of the love that renews all things."* Just as *"spring never fails in its task,"* your desire to be real ensures experience will never let you down.

When you are joyous of heart and content in thought, *"you can determine good fortune and misfortune on earth, and bring to perfection everything you see."* Good fortune is merely a pathway where nothing needs to be undone.

As you discover more, you suffer less. This is the sublimity of how nature brings perfection to the earth. The Master said: *"If you would have a thing laid aside, you must first set it up."* You are given the opportunity to block this joy or receive it, because it resides perpetually in your heart. Only you can allow it to roam free.

To lay aside your barriers, you must first "set them up" or come to understand how you block your ability to live joyfully. Cultivating a sense of joy that you carry wherever you go can become a way of living. Sometimes you must aim high, knowing that failure will always pull a little on your accomplishments, although one who meets all experience as an opportunity for growth never fails and always succeeds.

"Life is the refuge for the myriad creatures. It is that by which the good man protects; it is that by which, the bad is protected. Even if a man is not good, why should he be abandoned?" In the image of someone speaking and making things equal, Tui shows how life excels on bestowing and is always productive.

Accessing the transformative power of nature that resides in your core, contentment or discontentment is simply the measure of your joy in following. *"Rid the self of expectations to find the accidental environment where joy is manifesting."*

HUAN The Homecoming

59th Degree: *Life scatters to reunite; there is a thing confusedly formed.*

"There is a destiny that makes us brothers, no one goes his way alone;
All that we send into the lives of others comes back into our own."

– Edwin Markham

"After joy, comes dispersal. Dispersion means scattering." As a child, perhaps you played with dandelion pods, blowing their white, billowing seeds into the wind. Little did you realize the enormous complexity and beauty of a life form that harnesses the wind for regeneration.

Over 100,000 species of mammals, insects and birds go about their daily routines, inadvertently transferring seeds or pollen grains from the male variety of one plant to the female variety of another. Why would nature devise such a complicated system of reproduction? If you were to view life as one giant organism, you would discover many checks and balances that amount to an all or nothing equation.

The wellness of nature's individual parts relies on the well-being of the whole. The Master said: *"If this was not the most divine thing on the earth, how could it do this?"*

The sublime complexity of nature creates symbiotic processes in which each species thrives in each other's presence. Herbivores need plants; carnivores depend on herbivores, and predation keeps a natural balance. Without scavengers like bacteria, waste could not be regenerated into plants. Without the rainforests and carbon consuming algae that cover the oceans, animals would be deprived of oxygen. At the same time that life is broken up, you can observe how it is regenerated through a reuniting. Huan is the image of how life scatters to expand. In this, *"there is a thing confusedly formed."*

"Intangible and elusive, yet within it is an image.
Elusive and intangible, yet within it is a form.
Deep and obscure, yet within it is an essence.
The essence is very real, and therein,
is something that can be tested.
From the ancient times until now,
its manifestations have never ceased."

When you open to life's interconnectivity, you can observe nature performing at its best. *"How do we know what life wants of us? It embraces and benefits all. How do we know that it embraces all? Because it holds all in its possession and bestows all creatures with the gift of food."* Although you may take this simple benevolence for granted, it is actually quite profound.

When we observe the interdependency inherent in the natural world, we must wonder if we too, are scattered to reunite in some way that we have yet to understand. The Master said: *"My Way has one string which threads it all together."*

"The Firm comes and does not exhaust itself; the Yielding receives and what is above is in harmony with it." One who can appreciate nature's power for renewal, and would explore "harmony in one's greater relationship to life" will find a profound level of initiation on a pathway of environmental work. *"Whatever we do to the web, we do to ourselves."* To become a steward of just one small segment of life will create a chain reaction that reverberates across the entire tapestry, which always returns to make you stronger.

"Who can be muddy and yet, settling slowly come to life? Who can be at rest and yet, stirring slowly come to life? One who holds fast to the Tao of Nature."

Undefined and yet, complex; interdependent and inspired to drive each thing to be unique, nature finds harmony, even while it honors diversity. You can observe its tremendous power for renewal in the purposeful way that experience activates your inborn pattern of development. Observing this complicated chain of sustenance reveals that nature is not only your teacher, it is also your redeemer.

CHIEH Limitation

60th Degree: *Adaptation allows you to harmonize with the changes. Everything you will ever need can be found within.*

"Follow effective action with quiet reflection.
From the quiet reflection will come even more effective action."

– James Levin

"Things cannot be forever separate. Therefore follows limitation." The Abysmal Water over the Joyous Lake is an image of something inexhaustible being contained for use. Chieh portrays how you access an inexhaustible source within and yet, are able to give each experience definition. There is a danger however, that these definitions can come to limit your ability to grow. The process of adaptation demonstrates that limitations force creatures to harmonize with a changing world.

Opportunistic adaptation appears in the Yellow Jacket variety of wasps, which have come to resemble honeybees. Once their insect diet disappears in late summer, they often raid honeycombs to feed their appetite for sweets. Ravens have also developed an opportunistic relationship with wolves. They will cry out to alert wolves to potential prey, so that they too, can eat.

Limitations activate the adaptive response, which transformed the scales of some dinosaurs into feathers. We tend to associate feathers with flight, although many birds do not fly. While flight does aid survival, feathers evolved as an adaptive response and way of regulating body heat. Many reptiles still rely on shade and the warmth of the sun to adjust their temperature. The power of nature reveals how limitations drive the engine of evolution. Although you may grow frustrated with restrictions, limitations not only make you stronger, they also lead you forward.

Once, a farmer of sheep lived beside a man who owned hunting dogs. Every night the dogs broke through the farmer's fence and killed several of his sheep. The farmer complained to the neighbor on several occasions, although the situation never changed. In great frustration, he sought the advice of a judge who told the farmer that he could solve his problem, but only if the farmer promised to do what he suggested. The farmer agreed, but the judge told him to give the neighbor two of his best sheep! The farmer was outraged. Since he was a man of his word, he returned home and offered his neighbor two of his best sheep. The neighbor received this unexpected gift with suspicion. Knowing that the farmer was a man of his word, he thanked him and assumed that it was in return for his incessant complaining. The next morning, the farmer expected to find the usual broken fence and missing sheep, but all was well on his farm. Because the neighbor now had sheep to protect, he had built a fine enclosure for his hunting dogs.

When you adapt to the changes, you will begin to see harmony like a seed inherent in all discord. To harmonize with the changes, a shift in perspective makes what appears difficult, easy. Do not approach limitations as barriers, but see them as a springboard for discovery and innovation.

Nature uses limitations as a creative treasure trove to explore endless variations. By accessing the power of nature, you can rise to meet each challenge with the same innovative vision of growth. Your limitations will always be intrinsically tied to the development of your strengths.

CHUNG FU Inner Truth

61st Degree: *Do not seek to follow in the footsteps of the wise, seek what they sought.*

"Nature never says one thing
and wisdom another."

–Decimus Junius Juvenalis

"Through being limited, things are made dependable. Hence follows the image of inner truth." The neighbor was made dependable when he faced the same limitations as the farmer. The Wind blows over the Joyous Lake, while the Mountain and Thunder are stirring within. Chung Fu offers a message about achieving steady and joyous movement even while you open yourself to every possibility for renewal.

Chung Fu has two open lines within, which are surrounded by firm lines. This openness at the center reveals great power because *"a heart that remains open can be guided by inner truth."* Difficulty is always transformed when you can approach it like a question rather than an obstacle. *"A heart that is free of prejudice in meeting adversity will discover only favorable circumstances."*

To activate nature's transformative power within, you must remain objective when meeting the necessary tension that keeps life evolving. Do not fall prey to the illusion that when you reach the height of your inner truth, circumstances will not continue to further shape you. *"Be not sad,"* tension is the driving force of evolution.

In time, you will recognize that tension is evolving peace. Tranquility must then give way to further transformations. Moving Joyfully through life's fluctuating movement allows you to find comfort in the way of change.

Life continuously shakes you free from any stagnant way of thinking, even when you feel you are at your height. You may give in after a long struggle or endless defeat, and this "giving in" reveals how the pathway could not have been otherwise. Forced to make minor changes, these changes become significant to your success. This small shift in acceptance goes a long way in reducing anxiety. It is no simple thing to say: *"know contentment and you are rich."*

"Wind over the Lake: the image of inner truth." You may remember throwing stones into the Lake to observe how it moved in circular waves that rippled outward toward the shore. Even if you were to throw a rectangular block into the water, the waves would still move in perfect circles. This is because the *fabric* of water is not what it

appears to be. Its horizontal movement is an illusion; its molecules spin vertically and remain where they are. What appears as waves is the energy moving through the *fabric* of water. As each molecule spins, the water crests, although the molecules remain where they are.

When you observe people sitting in the bleachers at a football game, to create the wave, each one stands and throws their arms into the air in succession. Like the water molecule, they remain where they are, while the energy moves from one to another across the stadium.

Like the center of the molecule, Chung is the center out of which you evolve. Fu is how you hold to it, regardless of where the changes lead you. The energy of change can move you in different ways, although the core of who you are remains stationary. This center is awakened by the changes, and you must hold to it. You can observe your emotions as the waves or response to the movement of life flowing through you. Holding to your center actually makes life more joyful.

This center gives shape to your unique destiny when you can see how experience shapes it. Buffeted by events, you remain true to this center. Regardless of what you do, when you keep doing it, your actions will define your character. The force that keeps you connected to this center is your philosophy or inner truth.

"In the pursuit of learning, one knows more every day; in the pursuit of following life, one does less every day. One does less and less until one does nothing at all, and when one does nothing at all there is nothing that is undone." Chung Fu is an image of an arrow at the center of a target, with

a bird's claw encircling a hatchling. It offers the idea of both, capture and protection.

"When your discernment penetrates the four quarters, are you capable of not knowing anything?" Chung Fu suggests the subtle way that by holding to your center, you always hit the mark. The great claw becomes the image of how life protects you and holds you to this center.

HSIAO KUO Overwhelming of the Small

62nd Degree: *The weakest force is more powerful than gravity, and the smallest of life forms are the most successful. Appreciating what is small is called enlightenment.*

"I once had a sparrow alight on my shoulder
for a moment while I was hoeing in a village garden,
and I felt that I was more distinguished by that circumstance
than I should have been by any epaulet I could have worn."

– Thoreau

"When one has the trust of the creatures, one sets them in motion. Therefore, follows the overwhelming of the small." Like a spider, pursuing only what lands in its web, millions of jellyfish ride the ocean currents. They do not pursue, although their long tentacles trap plankton wherever they are led. Observing nature's smallest manifestations, you can observe the art form of life behaving powerfully in microscopic ways.

As one of the last principles in the Book of Changes, it is interesting that it focuses on the little things in life. The heart of Taoism rests in this respect for simplicity. When anything exceeds the mean, the result will always be a transitional state that arises from extraordinary conditions. The situation is extraordinary because the gathering energy is about to transform into something new. In this, Hsiao Kuo offers a message about the build up of energy from what appears to be insignificant.

The multi-cellular kingdom of plant-life across the earth and oceans, demonstrates the overwhelming power of the small. As the most prolific of all life forms, plants offer a picture of the great industry that takes place at the micro level. These are our ancestors and the root of our existence. *"In the perception of the smallest is the secret of clear vision."* In the things that you fail to see, life is teaching you the most.

Life's smallest creatures portray the ultimate power to succeed. Those who travel the least teach will teach you the most about existing "just so." When you are not moving, your unique unfolds from within. Overwhelming of the Small resembles a bird, and suggests a type of transition that warns you of losing your sense of remaining grounded. The Master said: *"The small bird brings the message: it is not well to strive upward. It is well to remain below."*

Activating the transformative power within, you will discover that *"striving upward is rebellion, striving downward is devotion."* Simplicity allows you to focus on cultivating your ability to follow, while traveling little helps you to remain steadfast. The smallest seed becomes an enormous tree by not striving *out there* but striving to develop its essence *in here.*

As the opposite of Inner Truth, there is a warning that striving upward can disconnect you from your center. You push upward to break through your barriers, although at times you must *"bow down for preservation."*

The longevity and flexibility of the insect world and plant kingdom can teach you about adaptability. Seeds find life in the most inhospitable environments. Some grow from oxygen alone, while others hitchhike on animal fur or on the wind to find a home. It is not *where they are going,* but *how they get there* that make them our teachers.

The Overwhelming of the Small offers a lesson about how you blossom because of the conditions that unfold around you, yet everything you will ever become grows from within. Cyclically, plants shed their growth and *"bow down to be preserved."* In this, you are reminded that life is not a constant flowering.

The need for restraint might appear excessive, but King Wen, imprisoned by the tyrant Chou Hsin, used his time in confinement to focus on the small matters that gave birth to his understanding of these sixty-four principles. Overwhelming of the Great suggested that the beam was excessive in weight and required support. Yet, Overwhelming of the Small is at the foundation of all of life.

"If the mind is not overlaid with wind and waves, you will always be living among blue mountains and green trees." Observing the power of the small, the Master said: *"this is why I know the benefit of resorting to no*

action; the Way shows no favoritism." Regardless of its size or behavior, all things are equal in the eyes of nature.

More importantly, you need not wave your arms in the air for life to notice you. *"You can deplete your vital energy on external things and wear out your spirit."* Just keep doing that which you feel you are being led to do. From the empire within, little ideas can lead to small actions; incessant thought and continual action leads to what you experience. No matter how small, the little things can become enormous over time. Only be vigilant in what you are doing in thought and action.

Like the plant, something profound takes root within, called forward by the changes taking place without. When you realize how life leads you to flower at the same time that you are replenished by turning within, your success is assured.

CHI CHI After Completion

63rd Degree: *Equilibrium is the great foundation of life, and harmony its universal path.*

"Voyager, there are no bridges;
one builds them as one walks."

– Gloria Anzaldua

"One who stands above things, brings them to completion. Water over fire: the condition after completion." Water always moves downward; fire always burns upward and eventually they will meet. There is an obvious threat that the Abysmal Water will extinguish the Clinging

Fire, or that the flame will lead to evaporation. In this way, Chi Chi presents the encounter that happens when the Profound comes up against the ideas we Cling to. Nothing in nature can remain in a state of equilibrium.

After Completion, the stage is set for a transition. Just when everything appears to be in order, the situation turns chaotic. At all levels of life, when order appears, it makes its transition to a new order through what appears to be disorder. The unknown has not emerged and all we know is that something has ended. At the end of summer, leaves shimmer on the trees, yet before they return to a fresh green color, we watch as they are swept away chaotically when autumn sets in. If we are ignorant to how nature regenerates itself, we might say that something is wrong when the world dies away. During a forest fire or torrential rains, nature dons the face of chaos.

During difficult transitions, it is hard to comprehend the reason for the change at hand. How do you explain to a person facing foreclosure that the transition was necessary? After Completion, all that is left is the truth; what worked in the past might not work in the future. Those living on a type of credit beyond their means must come to terms with the real value of *cash.* Markets are no different than the inward and outward expansion in the natural world. *"When anything reaches its extreme, it must turn back."*

Violent acts of frustration by the oppressed show how the low is lifted up. Institutions that thrive on dishonest practices discover how the high is brought down. When houses are no longer affordable, an adjustment in price is in order. One thing we can be certain of is that the truth always comes to light.

Approaching the conclusion to the Book of Changes, one immediately notices how the last two principles appear to be backwards. It would seem that After Completion should follow Before Completion. However, this principle describes both the certainty and uncertainty that arises after each ending.

Like the adaptive variations that remain dormant until we need them, we are prepared for the condition before it comes. If our journey is viewed as one of disappointment and pain, chances are, life has been attempting release us from the unnecessary things we cling to. The manner in which we meet circumstances determines what we will make of them. When we lose something, we return to the basics. By returning to the basics, we discover additional value in living.

Circumstances break us free of what no longer serves us; it strips away the unnecessary that may block what we may become. The harder we cling to the illusion of keeping to the status quo, the longer and more difficult the fall. However, when the dust settles, we usually discover the purpose for the change.

The Master said: *"Thus the sage takes thought of misfortune to arm against it in advance."* You are armed against misfortune by your willingness to recognize how situations evolve. This is the perpetuation of how disorder leads to order; it is also the natural way that order leads to disorder. Nothing in nature comes to completion; it moves toward renewal, and nothing comes to a standstill, it merely transforms.

Perhaps the principles were organized in this way to remind us that life is not linear, but is moving back and forth in an endless cycle of renewal. *"First good order prevails and in the end disorder."* This is simply how life moves toward harmony or dissolution, but the power of nature is always productive. Chi Chi takes shape as the only principle where all the lines are in their proper places, and it is the image where Peace or oblivion might lead to Standstill. After completion or standstill, we prepare for a time of renewal.

We are voyagers in a world that is perpetually changing. Yet, the changes that we face are always teaching us about ourselves. After Completion comes a time to approach what has already happened to understand what we can do to keep it from happening again. To access the transformative power of nature, adaptation becomes more than just a biological drive. Adaptation is also the conscious choices we make in the present that will come to shape our future. Evolution shows that natural selection strengthens the things that make our species successful. At all levels of life, if the approach allows us to thrive and grow, nature supports it; if not, circumstances force us to let go.

When we look at the power of nature, we wonder how humans could ever really affect it. We must remember that life is always teaching us something about *ourselves.*

The honeybee is the major pollinator of much of our agriculture. German scientists have found that their navigational capability, or "waggle dance" is interrupted by cellular telephone frequencies. At the same time that cellular signals are increasing across the world, bee colonies are disappearing at alarming rates. Cell phone activity may be causing bees to lose their ability to find their way back to the hive, and they just disappear.

Deciding between the importance of honeybees and cell phones is like choosing between paper and plastic in the grocery store. Progress can not be measured in only human terms, as nature ever reminds us: *"Nature treats the people like straw dogs."* In an instant, all we build can crumble. Progress sometimes requires that we go backward before moving forward. When we observe the changes taking place in nature, we discover we are no different.

We can usually only see the problem, after something happens, and life has a way of always reflecting the things that we need to learn. Climate change will not teach us about sustaining nature; we are learning a lesson about sustaining ourselves. Each of the principles reveals how something comes to undo what we tend to do.

The Doctrine of the Mean or Chung-Yung developed as an ancient Chinese study of adaptability and universal harmony. Chung is the center, while Yung is what is universal and harmonious. The "Mean" was the balance between human nature and its relationship to the whole. *The Doctrine of the Mean* reveals how people and nature must form a unity: *"equilibrium is the great foundation of the world, and harmony its universal path."*

"If one stands still at the end, disorder arises, because the Way comes to an end." Our way may come to an end, but Nature's Way moves ever onward.

WEI CHI Before Completion

64th Degree: *You are always on the threshold of change; how you approach it will determine your success.*

"We sometimes get all of the information,

but we refuse to get the message."

–Cullen Hightower.

"Things cannot exhaust themselves. Hence, follows at the end, the principle of before completion." After Completion revealed the highest order that inevitably gives way to disorder. Wei Chi embodies the opposite condition where disorder has already set in. The fact that it is the last principle in the Book of Changes reveals how comfortable the ancients were with the idea of a universe in constant flux. The Taoists did not share stories about creation because something that is always changing cannot be described as being created. In this principle, we discover the freedom required to embrace life's possibilities.

When disorder sets in, it can lead to a profound sense of hopelessness. Disorder and discontentment are the first signs that something powerful looms on the horizon.

Within disorder, we discover the seed, which will inevitably lead back to order. Where complacency often leads to stagnation, the tension of change is already at play, and it is better to follow where the changes might lead. At the height of disorder, there is great power in recognizing the shape of a new situation.

Stagnation can only evolve into Harmony once disorder moves toward exhaustion; Harmony moves toward Stagnation when order reaches its peak. *"When anything reaches the extreme, it must turn back."* In Wei Chi, we stand at the threshold of change and have the opportunity to learn from our mistakes. How we approach these changes will determine our success.

Chi Chi presented Water over Fire, and as its opposite, Wei Chi portrays Fire over Water. It would seem that since Fire burns upward and Water flows downward, there will be no connection between the two and the situation is hopeless. The fact that these two elements are moving in opposite directions is what makes the situation interesting and new. Anytime opposites appear, there will be a transformation.

The image of Fire moving upward portrays how we look for Synergy or meaning by reaching toward the heavens. All the time, the Abysmal releases its profound wisdom below and all around us. We look to the sky for answers when life is speaking to us daily, in a thousand different ways. When we come back to earth, it always hands us its calling card: *"This is your home....welcome back."* Anytime we travel around the world, we will find our way home because *it truly is round.*

We lose our connectivity to the earth when we believe our fate is in the hands of something arbitrary. As the Profound and Clinging Fire reconnect, we discover our deeper relationship to the earth

At Tsu Sang Hu's burial, a disciple was concerned to hear two young men singing and playing flutes.

"Do you think that it is appropriate to sing in the presence of a corpse?" He asked. The two looked at each other, and then at the corpse, laughing: *"What does he know about ceremony?"* It is far more important to be true to your nature and express what you feel, rather than do what you believe is correct, or expected of you. In this, we see how disorder or moving against the status quo can be a prerequisite for authenticity.

At all levels of life, a thousand miracles are taking place every moment, which we simply cannot see. We value our structures, but if they threaten our well-being, life will always move to free us from them. Water appeared when oxygen and hydrogen molecules came together. Their electrical distribution created an interesting tension that made an ocean. It took billions of years to perfect a process that initiated life on this planet. Chances are, nature's productive logic is more capable of ensuring your success than we realize.

The Master said: *"How do we know that what we call heaven is not actually man, and that what we call man is not actually heaven?"*

Fire below gets water moving energetically. Yet, even without heat, water will still form into perfect crystals. In life, at some degree, everything is in continual motion. Wei Chi is the image of outward disorder that can lead to a sense of hopelessness, yet over and over, we recognize how order pre-arranges itself out of apparent chaos. Just as unhappiness signals how authenticity emerges, disorder is the only pathway to suppleness and renewal.

Regardless of the form the Changes take, life has a special predisposition for generating disorder; *it is a prerequisite in its pursuit of a better way. "Be not sad,"* it also has fondness for orchestrating order. Perhaps that is why everything always seems to work out, whether we choose to worry about it or not.

"Although the lines are not in their proper places, the firm and yielding correspond." We see this in the movement of electricity, atoms, gravity, pressure systems and in the building blocks of life.

Since nothing can reach completion, the trend moves toward the opposite condition: renewal.

Within life's complex processes, we are brought toward harmony and dissolution in the same way that substances change, or how forces collide, harmonize and eventually transform.

Like waves moving back and forth from one shoreline to another, we detect life's gentle thread that ripples in a chain of sustenance from one species to another. Whether we view life at the molecular level, or nature's symbiotic economies of survival, everywhere we look, we discover profound diversity, symmetries and meaningful design. Why nature should propel itself toward the pursuit of excellence does not have to remain a mystery. *Nothing Bad Happens in Life* when we meet life with the change in perspective that the time demands. *"The truth is not a sign that points to something beyond itself, it just is."*

We are an integral part of life's tapestry and the fact that we can appreciate its innate complexities makes us unique, but in no way more special. Nature reveals its enormous power to sustain and strengthen its creatures to those who would follow its ways. Although the *Book of Changes* ends with the idea of disorder, we know that it is a necessary pathway to renewal. The Synergistic Flame over the Profound returns us to our symbiotic connection to the truth of what unfolds around us.

As the transition arrives, we see the image of the tree before it begins to branch. In between the stagnation of winter and the great fullness of summer is spring: a rebirth. Out of apparent nothingness, something new emerges. We know it will come again, because it has come before.

The situation is strange and new, the past is a world away, and we are ripe for a transformation. Once things reach the end, we can approach the opportunity to blossom anew.

There is an ancient story that the rainbow is a symbol of our well-being. This may well be true because as it arc across the sky, it reveals the round way of things we may never see.

CPSIA information can be obtained at www.ICGtesting.com
Printed in the USA
LVOW10s1443150616

492730LV00001B/79/P